WHERE WILTSHIRE MEETS SOMERSET

20 Best Walks in the Country around Bath, Bradford on Avon,
Trowbridge, Westbury, Warminster & Frome

Roger Jones

Illustrations by Edward Dowden
Maps by Karen Pigott

Where Wiltshire Meets Somerset

First published in 1982
This revised, reset and redesigned
edition published in 1998 by
EX LIBRIS PRESS
1 The Shambles
Bradford on Avon
Wiltshire

Design and typesetting by Ex Libris Press

Covers printed by Shires Press, Trowbridge

Printed and bound by
Cromwell Press, Trowbridge

ISBN 0 948578 94 7

*Previous pages: Cley Hill and Corsley Church
Cover: Gateway below Farleigh Castle (Walk 20),
water colour by Edward Dowden*

CONTENTS

CONTENTS

Introduction

When I came to live in Bradford on Avon in the summer of 1980 I set about exploring the countryside around the town at my first opportunity. I had lived in South Devon for four years at a spot within easy reach of both the Coast Path and Dartmoor National Park, so I was rather spoilt for beauty and variety in my walking.

My first walks out of Bradford were along the towpath of the Kennet and Avon Canal towards Avoncliff, where I found a country as attractive as much in South Devon. Here the River Avon flows through a steep-sided valley which is garlanded with woods and studded with villages built from the stone of the hills on which they stand. The prospect of Bradford from Barton Farm is very striking, particularly in the morning when the risen sun casts its light directly onto the terraces stacked one above the other on the south-east facing slope. The natural stone shines brilliantly, almost magically, as though it were somehow lit from within.

Turleigh is set high in a cleft on the north bank of the Avon and is followed by Avoncliff, set lower in the valley close by the mills which were once active on both banks. Farther down-river come Freshford and Limpley Stoke. These are all pleasant villages yet I remain especially attracted to the point where the Rivers Frome and Avon unite, where the Frome valley from the south widens to meet the Avon from the east. The stone bridge by The Inn at Freshford, the verdant meadows on the flood plain of the two rivers, the wooded eminence of Staples Hill: all combine to present a vision of great charm and tranquillity. At my first visit there I found the prospect up the Frome valley a great lure. Soon afterwards, as I pressed on along the canal towards Dundas Aqueduct, the valley of the Midford Brook appeared equally enticing.

We had moved into a house in the north-east corner of Bradford on Avon. As Woolley Street rises towards Woolley Green, the houses are replaced by fields which slope away to the south-east, across a wide vale in which Trowbridge is situated, and on towards the chalk escarpment of Salisbury Plain. The White Horse is visible from here, unless obscured by the plume of smoke from the cement works just below. Depending on the weather and the position of the sun, the chalk escarpment can appear very dramatic: like a great tidal wave suddenly frozen in its path westwards, and always as a most prominent feature in the landscape.

The hillside upon which much of old Bradford stands is composed of the creamy yellow limestone of which the Cotswold Hills and its towns and villages are made. A cursory examination of a geological map of the area assured me that, geologically speaking at least, Bradford on Avon stands on the slope of a hill that forms the south-eastern edge of the Cotswold range. It is interesting to note that the topographical writer, H.J. Massingham, in his book *Cotswold Country* (Batsford, 1937), deals with the limestone belt which outcrops in ten counties between Dorset and Lincolnshire. Massingham recognised the diversity yet underlying unity of that limestone belt, or 'Cotswold Country', in terms of geology, landscape and building materials.

The western scarp of Salisbury Plain was another feature beckoning me, and so naturally were the towns which lie at its feet, namely Trowbridge, Westbury and Warminster. The Somerset-Wiltshire border runs more or less north-south a few miles to the west of this string of towns, and even nearer to Bradford on Avon. I followed the valleys of the River Frome and the Midford Brook as they cross the county boundary into Somerset and I am quite convinced that the countryside changes in doing so. On the Somerset side the country seems more broken, more closely divided into hill and vale, somehow more intimate and more like the South Devon with which I was familiar. The Wiltshire side seems characterised more by open spaces, whether upland or lowland.

Cley Hill is an outpost of the Wiltshire chalk just north of the Longleat estate from which one can see Warminster to the east and Frome in Somerset to the west, or north-west and, beyond it, the Mendips. It seemed natural that I should extend my wanderings to Frome and its surroundings. After an initial visit to the town I was hooked. It has a charm and attractiveness totally different to that of

Bradford or the other towns of West Wiltshire. Until the removal of the livestock market to an out of town site in 1990, it had been a town unique among them. It was as important a centre of the wool and clothing trades as Bradford and Trowbridge, and has the fascinating Trinity area of artisans' houses built in the seventeenth and eighteenth centuries. This industrial housing is far removed from the drab rows of identical dwellings which were the norm during the industrial revolution of a later century.

It was during this time that the clothing industry, which was the staple of Frome's prosperity, was lost to the new centres of production in the north of England. This means that, like Bradford, Frome was never much affected by Victorian expansion and redevelopment and both towns maintain the appearance and atmosphere of an earlier era. Frome lacks the architectural riches of Bradford but has instead all manner of interesting backwaters, as befits an old market town.

In the triangle between Frome, Bath and Bradford on Avon there lies a relatively sparsely populated hinterland which is largely dependent on agriculture but which harbours such interesting and attractive villages as Lullington, Wellow and Norton St. Philip, all of which are well worth exploring.

In the area dealt with in this book, we find a diversity of landscape represented by the borders of the Mendips, the Cotswolds and Salisbury Plain, three geologically distinct upland areas. The River Avon rises in the Cotswolds and initially follows the dip of those hills in an easterly direction. Unlike her sister streams, which continue eastwards to join the Thames, the Avon flows through Malmesbury Vale, via Chippenham and Melksham, and then cuts back through the limestone strata of the 'geological Cotswolds' on its way to the Bristol Channel.

The River Biss, which springs up below the porous chalk strata of Salisbury Plain and which flows by Westbury and through Trowbridge, meets the Avon just up-river from Bradford. Down from Bradford, the Avon is joined by the River Frome which rises in eastern Mendip, and later by the Midford Brook, which is born of the Cam Brook and Wellow Brook, both of which flow from the Mendip foothills. These rivers and streams and their respective tributaries constituted an essential basis of the wool and cloth industries which have been such an important factor in the growth of the towns and villages in the area here described.

I had originally intended to consider the whole of the boundary where Somerset meets Wiltshire, extending farther south towards Mere in Wiltshire and Bruton in Somerset. However, the Longleat and Stourhead estates constitute a barrier to ramblers on the Wiltshire side and I felt that to include this extension southwards would expand the scope of the book to an unmanageable degree. Not only that, but there are sufficient variety and sources of interest in the area here defined, coupled with an historic unity represented by six hundred years of the wool and clothing trades to provide a suitable country for exploration.

Roger Jones
The Old Ship
Bradford on Avon
1998

Walking in the Countryside

Walking, I am convinced, is the only way to truly appreciate the countryside. The great advantage of walking as a means of getting about the country is its complete flexibility. By that I mean you can go at the pace you choose and, providing you stick to rights of way, you can stop exactly where and when you wish, in order to examine some building or natural feature which presents itself, or simply to admire the view.

I always look forward to setting out on a country walk, and especially that moment when I step off the concrete highway and on to a grassy track or perhaps a field path. Quite suddenly the din and stink of the traffic fades away and the natural sounds take over: the bird song, the wind in the trees, the sound of one's own footfall. Somehow it is a completely different world.

If we wish to walk, where can we do so? In the area where Wiltshire meets Somerset, there are a number of country lanes, green roads and field paths from which we can gain an inside view of the countryside. The ancient network of public footpaths and other rights of way is not as complete as it once was. The reason for this is quite simple. Before the age of motor transport, those who lived and worked on farms and in villages had usually to walk to get anywhere. Not that people went very far. Perhaps to the village church on a Sunday or to the nearest market town once a week to sell their produce.

A cursory glance at any large-scale Ordnance Survey map will reveal that the majority of footpaths and minor tracks provide shortcuts from farm to main road, from road to village. Pedestrians always found the shortest route to suit their, as a rule, very local orbit, and it was natural that they should ignore lanes and roads when there was a shorter route across fields or between hedgerows. Many of these old ways became increasingly neglected in the period after the First World War when motor transport became more widespread. This tendency has been even more marked in the twenty or thirty years after World War II. Former rights of way across agricultural land have sometimes been ploughed up and lost without trace, others that have been considered inconvenient or otherwise undesirable by farmers and landowners have been rendered inaccessible by some means or other. I have sometimes encountered public footpath notices which have been broken down, tracks between double hedgebanks which have had trees felled across them or mountains of rubbish dumped along their course. There are, too, problems presented in deciphering O.S. maps which have been rendered obsolete when farmers bulldoze hedges to enlarge fields, or pipe streams under ground to improve land drainage.

Yet one can understand the farmer's point of view. Gone are the days when he and his workers used the field paths; now that they no longer have any practical use for country folk, asks the farmer, why should ignorant townsfolk come and trample his crops. I have more than once been engaged in such a discussion with farmers after they had informed me that a public footpath no longer exists across their land and have been sent back the way I came. Yet what remains of our system of footpaths is surely worth protecting. Some town and parish councils and local branches of the Ramblers' Association undertake the task of regularly walking all the rights of way in their areas so that local landowners cannot apply for their closure. There can surely be no objection to people using these footpaths providing they do so with respect and observe the Country Code by closing gates and avoiding all risk of fire. In the long term, the farming community must stand to gain from an increased public awareness of the value of the countryside. It is a precious heritage which belongs to us all; it provides food for the spirit as well as the body.

Having walked all the routes in preparation for this new edition of *Where Wiltshire Meets Somerset* during the winter of 1997/8, I have been delighted at what good condition all the rights of way are in, and how well signposted the routes are. There is no doubt that the situation has improved enormously since I first researched this book in the early 1980s. Rambling is hugely popular today, and local authorities have woken up to the fact that the local network of footpaths is an invaluable resource and their maintenance is a good investment for the tourist industry. Wiltshire County Council Environmental Services, for example, publishes a regular News Sheet which details all the many repairs and improvements which have been enacted to public rights of way in the county over the previous months. Much of this work is carried out by local branches of the Ramblers Association and I am sure we are all grateful to both the volunteers and the paid professionals for all their good work.

A fairly substantial network of footpaths exists near the centres of population, for example around Frome and Bradford on Avon, and in the places generally recognised as beauty spots such as Vallis Vale and the Limpley Stoke valley. There are other areas, relatively far from towns and with unspectacular scenery, such as the hinterland around Norton St Philip, where many footpaths have disappeared or are unusable. Nevertheless, as partial compensation for the dearth of footpaths, there are many miles of lanes and minor roads along which very little traffic is encountered and which provide suitable routes for walkers.

I have walked all the footpaths included here and I have also checked them out with the relevant County authorities as being still legally accessible as public rights of way. There are times when it is not easy to keep strictly to public rights of way, particularly when paths cross open fields which have been ploughed or which are waist-high in corn. In such cases it is advisable to make a detour around the edge of the field in order to avoid trampling down crops or negotiating the ridge and furrow of a freshly ploughed field.

I am not one to go for a country ramble equipped as though I were planning to climb Everest but it should be remembered that, even in the driest weather, you are likely to encounter some mud and that, following a wet spell, it is as well to wear waterproof boots. Beware, too, of footpaths in the summer overgrown with brambles and stinging nettles – you will suffer greatly if you wear shorts!

Each of the walks described below is accompanied by an appropriate sketch map to show the route taken and the main features to be seen. The maps, together with the detailed description, should be sufficient to guide the rambler. However, anyone with a serious interest is recommended to acquire the relevant Ordnance Survey maps. These are as follows:

Landranger Series 1: 50, 000
(All public rights of way are shown in red):
Sheet 172: Bristol and Bath
Sheet 173: Swindon and Devizes
Sheet 183: Yeovil and Frome
Sheet 184: Salisbury and the Plain

Pathfinder Series 1: 25, 000
These larger scale maps show all rights of way in green, as well as all field boundaries. They are very clear and are excellent maps to use in the field.
Sheet 1183: Bath and Keynsham
Sheet 1184: Melksham
Sheet 1199: Radstock and Wellow
Sheet 1200: Westbury and Trowbridge
Sheet 1219: Frome and Shepton Mallet
Sheet 1220: Warminster and Area

Note: At the time of writing (winter 1997/8), the Pathfinder series is in the process of being superseded by the recently introduced Explorer series. These new maps are drawn to the same scale as the Pathfinders and contain just as much information but each covers twice the area of its predecessor, and costs only slightly more.

Explorer Series 1:25, 000
Sheet 155: Bristol and Bath
Sheet 5: Mendip Hills East

The Walks

Guide to Maps

The sketch maps accompanying the rambles in this book, together with the directions given in the text will, we trust, provide a sufficient guide even to the intending walker.

Key to the maps is as follows:

Route along lane, road

Route along track

Route along footpath

- **Note**
- In the text, passages giving directions are flagged on the
- left by a dotted line, as shown here.

1 AVONCLIFF

via Freshford, Iford and Westwood

Distance:	4 miles
Maps:	Pathfinders 1199, 1200
	Explorer 155
	Landrangers 172, 173
Map reference:	804599
Refreshment en route:	The Cross Guns pub at Avoncliff;
	The Inn at Freshford;
	Teazels Tea Shop at Avoncliff.

THE WALK is a splendid one by the banks of the Rivers Avon and Frome through a peaceful and delicious countryside. The gorge-like valley at Avoncliff opens out downstream where the Avon is joined by the Frome. The valley from Freshford to Iford is open meadow in its lower reaches, but wooded on its sloping sides. The mellow stone of the bridge, manor house and Italianate gardens at Iford contrasts delightfully with the verdure of the valley. There is a steep hill to climb from Iford up to Westwood and from Upper Westwood down again to Avoncliff.

Avoncliff is reached by road from Bradford on Avon or Westwood. From Bradford you take the Belcombe Road which forks left to follow the railway. The road ends at Avoncliff where there is some parking space by the canal. From Upper Westwood there is a lane which descends steeply down to the canal where a car park may be found to the left.

Avoncliff is a small but diverse community. There are the remains of two mills, facing one another on the banks of the Avon; there has been much quarrying and mining of Bath Stone in the hillsides around Avoncliff and, even today, there is a stone mine close by at Upper Westwood. The Kennet and Avon Canal and the railway both pass through Avoncliff, the former crosses the river and railway by a majestic, if crumbling, aqueduct and the railway even has a halt here. There is a pub, The Cross Guns, with a terrace which looks out onto the aqueduct and weir, and several houses scattered about the river, canal and railway. Access by road, however, is restricted, and only footpaths serve to reach points down-river towards Freshford and up the hill opposite the pub to Turleigh and Winsley.

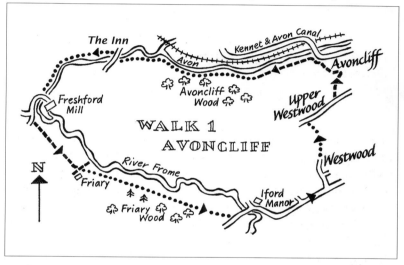

The mills formed part of the Hungerford Estate in the late fifteenth century and were used for grinding corn and fulling wool, though they were latterly employed as flock mills, finally closing down at the outbreak of the Second World War. Ancliff Square is a handsome edifice consisting of a continuous group of three-storey buildings facing a courtyard on three sides, all restored during the late 1980s and now occupied as private dwellings. Ancliff Square was formerly known as The Old Court and was so named during the nineteen-twenties when used as a hotel. Before the First World War it housed the Bradford Union Workhouse though its origin predates the Poor Law Act. It was built around 1800; its original purpose is not clear but it is generally accepted that it had some connection with the cloth trade, possibly comprising weavers' workshops and accommodation. There is a domed drying house still standing behind the main building.

To begin the walk, make for the footpath which passes under the aqueduct, in the same direction as the flow of the river, on the pub side. You pass by Ancliff Square on the left and continue by a well-worn footpath which is hedged on both sides and slightly elevated above the meadow beside the river on the right.

You reach a stile which leads you into a field — the path now follows a course close by the river. Traverse the meadow until you reach a stile where the hanging woods sweep down to the river bank. This stile also marks the point where Wiltshire meets Somerset. The woods soon end at a kissing gate where you enter a field — here you follow the beaten footpath across the field towards Freshford Bridge and The Inn to the right. The river which flows under Freshford Bridge is the Frome; the Frome joins the Avon just before the railway viaduct down-river.

Cross Freshford Bridge and enter a field on the left by a kissing gate to follow a signposted Public Footpath. After about fifty yards the right of way ascends the wooded slope on the right. Follow the footpath up the hill fairly steeply until you reach a kissing gate. If you bear right here you reach Freshford village, which is worth exploring sometime. But to continue the walk, bear left down the hill again towards the river. The hillside here slopes fairly precipitously and there is an old iron fence to protect the walker for the first section.

You eventually descend to the level of the river and leave the woods to enter a field by a stile. Carry on in the same direction towards the mills ahead and cross another stile to reach the lane.

Freshford Mill was originally the property of Hinton Charterhouse Priory and, after the dissolution, fell into the hands of a Trowbridge clothier. It continued as a cloth mill, and latterly as a flock mill, under various owners and tenants, until the Second World War. After the war it was used for the manufacture of rubber products.

Follow the lane upstream, beside the river, and take the first turning on the left towards Dunkirk Mill.

Dunkirk Mill dates from the eighteenth century and, after standing empty since 1912, was converted into a dwelling house in the 1980s.

Opposite the main entrance to Dunkirk Mill is a track crossing a field between fences. Follow this track to a tiny settlement in a cleft reaching down to the valley known as Friary (here were sited quarters for the lay brothers from nearby Hinton Priory). Step across the brook, then bear a few yards left before continuing in the same direction towards a gate. Enter a field and cross it by the left-hand edge towards a gate in the woods opposite. After a couple of hundred yards the right of way forks left down to a meadow. You now bear right to enjoy an unimpeded stretch of field path before reaching the lane at Iford. Don't miss looking back towards the Avon. Bear left to cross the bridge to Iford Manor.

Iford House and bridge

Iford Manor has an attractive early eighteenth century façade, though parts of the house are much older. The buildings on the left, with the fine oriel window, are the former stables, now converted into a pair of cottages. The gardens, with cloisters and colonnade and many fragments of ancient sculpture collected mainly from Italy, are quite unexpected along this quiet stretch of the River Frome.

Iford Manor is listed in the Domesday Book; it was purchased by Sir Thomas Hungerford in 1369, whose family held it for three centuries. In 1899 Iford was acquired by the architect Harold Peto, who set about creating his unique garden on this favourable south-facing slope. The gardens are regularly open in the summer months, including the Iford Arts Festival, when a booklet on the manor and gardens is available.

The picturesque Iford Bridge is of medieval origin and is supposed to have been built by the Carthusian monks from Hinton Charterhouse around 1400; Mr. Peto erected the figure of Britannia.

Bear right at Iford Manor up the rather steep hill by the lane towards Westwood. You reach the road by the gatehouse to Iford. Bear right and then left into the modern estate ironically named The Pastures. Bear left at the bottom beside the bungalow by a metalled pathway which leads to a stile whose appearance suggests it was there when The Pastures really were the pastures.

Climb the stile and turn right, past a chapel and a large house called Greenhill, towards a terrace of two-storey houses with long front gardens on the left. Just before this terrace turn left by the pavement on the right and past the entrance to Westwood Stone Mine. Follow the pavement until the public footpath is signposted along a narrow way. Follow this onwards and downwards – you encounter various crosstracks but simply keep to the most obvious, direct path until you emerge at the metalled lane. Here you turn left to descend to Avoncliff.

Norman north doorway at All Saints Church, Lullington (Walk 2)

2 BECKINGTON

via Rode, Woolverton, Laverton and Lullington

Distance:	5.5 miles
Maps:	Pathfinders 1199, 1200
	Explorer 155
	Landrangers 172, 173
Map Reference:	801518
Refreshment en route:	The Red Lion at Woolverton,
	The Woolpack Inn at Beckington

THE WALK passes through five diverse villages. Most of the walking is by field paths although there is a stretch of lane between Woolverton and Laverton, but you are unlikely to encounter much traffic there. An ancient track takes you west from Rode to cross the River Frome by Scutt's Bridge, a former pack horse bridge, unwidened and accessible only on foot, like the bridge at Tellisford a little further down-river (Walk 13)

The cross-country walking between villages will surely convince you that there really is no better way to appreciate a rural landscape than on foot; the route from Woolverton via Laverton, Lullington and back to Beckington has a refreshingly remote feel about it, and is really quite surprising in this respect.

Beckington may be familiar to many who live in the district where Somerset meets Wiltshire as a large village lying astride the junction of two main roads: the A36 Bath-Warminster and the A361 Frome-Trowbridge roads. The new bypass opened in 1989 and has restored Beckington to a peace which almost predates the motor age.

The village main street is wide and you should have no problem parking your car.

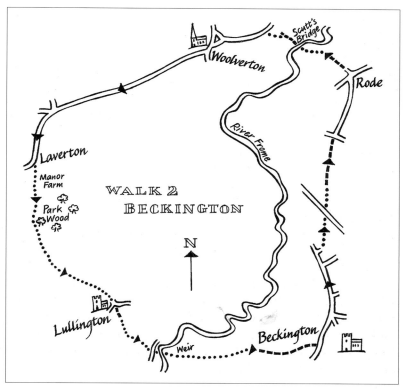

A perambulation of Beckington is well worth the effort and, without the traffic, is much more enjoyable than it used to be; the village boasts a wealth of fine stone buildings and an interesting church.

If you wish to see more of Beckington before setting out on the circular walk, make for Church Street, which leaves the main road to the left a little beyond the Woolpack Inn. St. George's Church stands handsomely in its churchyard, and its most impressive feature – a fine Norman tower – at once captures your attention. Inside, the church contains much of interest. There are several monuments, including one on the west wall to Samuel Daniel the poet, who died in 1619. There is a piscina, a timbered roof above clerestory windows and several fine corbel heads.

Bear left at the churchyard gate and walk on to Beckington Castle, a three-storeyed, sixteenth-century mansion with three gables facing the street and a castellated porch and stair turret at the side. Bear right here by the former main road (now a cul de sac) and right again at the present road. Opposite is the entrance to Stubbs Lane where the conical roof of a little gazebo marks the boundary wall of Beckington House, a three-gabled house set back from the road. Cross the road and bear left. Just below is a most attractive Baptist Chapel dated 1786 and, beyond that, on the same side, a former coaching inn, now a private house, where the iron support of the inn's name board still projects from the wall.

Baptist Church, Beckington

Back on the main road you can see The Grange and Beckington Abbey on the opposite side, parts of which date from the sixteenth century – these buildings have ecclesiastical origins though details are obscure. Continue through the village, past many old and attractive houses. Beckington is a sizeable village and its many substantial houses bear witness to a former prosperity founded on the wool trade.

To begin the walk: At the northern fringe of Beckington you reach a road junction with the road to Trowbridge to the right. Continue northwards here, past Beckington Memorial Hall. Just before the row of houses ahead cross a stile beside a gate on the right which leads into a field. Once past the gardens of these houses head for a wooden stile in the bottom left corner. Follow the hedgerow on your right. Pretty soon you reach the northerly extension of the Beckington bypass, and a double step stile beside the road. Climb over and prepare to cross the road. You may have to wait a while for a break in the traffic but you have a good long view in either direction so when you get your chance – run for it!

On the far side drop down just beyond the crash barrier and bear right to reach a similar wooden stile. Cross here and follow the hedgerow on the right until you reach an old kissing gate. Go through this to reach a lovely tree-lined path which you follow to reach a minor junction of lanes. Carry straight on for Rode. The River Frome flows unseen in the valley to your left, the spire of Woolverton Church may be seen above the far bank.

Bear right on reaching the southern outskirts of Rode, then turn sharp left. Once past the houses on your right, the road abruptly reverts to a tree-lined track and leads down towards the River Frome. As the way levels out, look out for a kissing gate on your left. Once through here it is interesting to observe the fallen masonry and disused channels just ahead. You can see the stone-lined walls of a former mill leat which supplied the Rockabella clothing factory which once occupied the site.

Follow the course of the former mill stream on the right, until you reach a bridge, indicated by a Public Footpath sign, which leads to the narrow, three-arched packhorse bridge, known as Scutt's Bridge, across the River Frome.

Just up-river from Scutt's Bridge, a single-span stone bridge crosses a mill stream which at this point returns to the river, having been diverted to supply the former Scuttsbridge Mill, now demolished.

Cross Scutt's Bridge and continue by the track ahead. Bear left at the lane and walk on into Woolverton, taking the left fork at the Red Lion. Woolverton Church is set back from the main road and, while of no special interest, is attractive enough in its flowery, walled churchyard.

On leaving the church, turn right at the main road, then right again for the lane to Laverton. After about half a mile there is a crosstrack, the northern section of which represents a short piece of the Poole-Bath Roman road; the southern section became the old Henhambridge Way.

Take the left fork ahead and descend to Laverton which has its own church, St. Mary's, but which is really little more than a hamlet. Leave the road and walk through the churchyard to the far side. Cross the fence into a yard surrounded by farm buildings.

Bear left and follow the Public Footpath signs to a stile; cross here and turn right, as indicated. Leave the field by a gate, cross the track and climb the stile opposite to continue along the bottom of the next field beside the stream on your left until you meet a stile leading to a stone slab bridge across the stream.

Bear right. The field narrows where it meets a wood on the left. Cross a stile to reach a further stile in the very far corner where you enter the wood, albeit briefly.

You emerge into a field. Now follow the hedgebank on your right until it swings off to the left. Here you go through the gap on the right, then bear left and head across the field towards a small clump of trees which encloses a pond. Carry on to reach the 5-bar wooden gate in the corner. From here you have a good view of Lullington. Head across the field to reach a stile in the far left corner. Cross here and bear left past a barn, then right past the farmhouse and church.

Lullington is a most attractive small village with a gem of a Norman church at its centre. All Saints has a splendid northern doorway (see page 21) which can easily be missed if you do not walk right round the church but merely enter by the south door. The plan of the church is unusual in that the tower is at the centre, between the nave and chancel. Inside, the columns at the four corners of the tower are most elaborate and make a fascinating study. The church

LULLINGTON

also contains an inscribed and much decorated Norman font. Lullington village is quiet and well preserved although the school is now a house and there is neither shop nor pub.

Bear left past the village pump, and thatched cottages, then right at a traditional red telephone box and down a metalled track. Just before the house ahead bear right to cross a stream via a pair of signposted gates to follow the stony path beside the trees to the left. The grounds of Orchardleigh House are to the right, now, inevitably, converted into a golf course. As you cross the metalled driveway to the house look to the left for a view of the somewhat over-the-top gatehouse.

Look out for a signpost on the left at the end of the line of trees. Bear left here to leave the stony track and follow a beaten path beside the stream which takes you down towards the River Frome. You reach a lane by a stile. Cross over the stile opposite, then bear right towards the footbridge which spans the River Frome.

Head straight across the field towards a stile on the far side. Make for the stile to the right (the far right) of the farmhouse ahead, then head towards the stile in the far right hand corner of the next field. Now walk straight on until you reach a stile which drops you onto Stubbs Lane. Carry on for Beckington village where you emerge on the main street beside the gazebo which marks the boundary wall of Beckington House.

3 BRATTON CASTLE

via Upton Cow Down, Old Dilton and Westbury White Horse

Distance:	7.5 miles
Maps:	Landrangers: 183,184
	Pathfinders: 1200, 1220
Map reference:	901515
Refreshment en route:	The Bell at Chalford on the A350, positioned just before the last leg of the walk

THE WALK is a longish but exhilarating one. The path from Bratton Castle along the chalk scarp is exposed and windswept and the bare downs afford little protection against the elements. It is advisable to choose a clear, sunny day for this walk as the views are far and wide. Bratton Castle is an impressive Iron Age hill fort which encloses a long barrow of the Bronze Age. It is pretty certain that the Battle of Ethundun, described in the *Anglo-Saxon Chronicle* as the battle at which King Alfred defeated the Danes, took place near here, by the village of Edington which lies under the scarp to the north-east. Tradition has it that the White Horse was cut to commemorate the great victory, though others argue that it dates only from the early eighteenth century. The redundant and unique church at Old Dilton provides a haven of rest after the stiff walk across open down.

Bratton Castle may be approached from Bratton village or from Westbury. In either case park in the designated areas under the south-facing ramparts.

To begin the walk, make for the metalled track which runs along the top of the scarp away from Bratton Castle and in a south-westerly direction (towards Westbury). At the crossroads carry straight on.

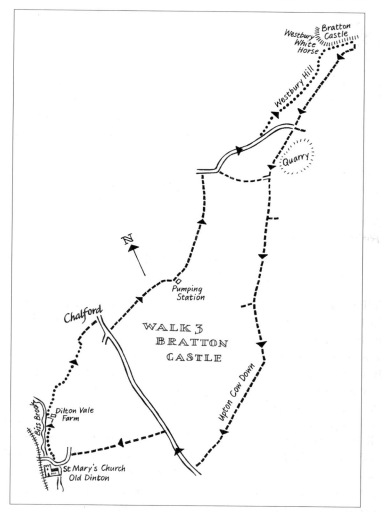

Immediately on your left is the entrance to a working chalk quarry, signposted Blue Circle Cement: Westbury Chalk Quarry. Here chalk is removed to provide one of the raw materials for the cement works situated below the Castle. You can get a good view of the enormous hole in the chalk from the track a little farther on. The vertical walls of the quarry give an excellent cross-section through the near horizontal chalk strata, distinguished by lines of flint nodules. The quarried chalk is crushed and mixed with water and the resultant slurry is pumped by underground pipeline to the nearby factory. Here the chalk is mixed with clay which is dug from the ground adjacent to the works; the mixture is then baked in kilns to make cement.

Continue along the high, straight track. Your way now is quite unmistakable. Simply carry on along the stony track, ignoring all footpaths and bridleways signposted to right and left. (This scarp-top is currently signposted as the Imber Range Path). After about a mile the track deviates slightly from its direct course, first left and then right, to negotiate the eminence of Upton Cow Down whose summit is marked at 199 metres on the Pathfinder map.

There are firing ranges within earshot to the left and official notices warning of the danger of same. However, the track ahead is a designated right of way and some distance from the rat-tat-tat of gunfire. Ahead looms the village of Upton Scudamore with the instantly recognizable blister of Cley Hill beyond. As the track descends from a high point near the summit you have a lovely view across a dry valley and into the rather wild hinterland of Salisbury Plain, towards the lost village of Imber, though the last is not visible from here.

As the path descends keep your eyes peeled for a 6-bar metal gate on the left, about a hundred yards above the clearing at the bottom of the track. Hop on to the bank directly opposite the gate and follow a beaten path which at first runs parallel to the track and then veers off to the right.

Soon this path will drop you on to the former course of the A350, now redundant since the new road was built some years ago. This old road now provides a hazard-free means of reaching the next stage of the route. You reach a point where the old road ends and a Bridleway sign points across the main road.

The A350 is always a busy road so great care should be taken before crossing. Once across you pass through a gate to follow a straight track across fields towards Old Dilton Farm.

> *Bear left at Old Dilton Farm down the lane through the Greensand, now characteristically sunken, which leads past houses and across a bridge over the infant Biss Brook to St. Mary's Church, whose low roof line and bell turret stand cheek by jowl with the railway bridge and embankment behind.*

St. Mary's was declared redundant in 1973 and is now maintained under the Redundant Churches Fund. The perpendicular exterior, with its bell turret and variety of windows, leads to an even more unexpected interior. The nave and north aisle contain an entirely unspoilt eighteenth century interior where every available space has been utilised for the erection of box pews, some of which incorporate medieval pews and parts of a former screen.

St. Mary's Church, Old Dilton

Above all rises a grand three-decker pulpit complete with sounding board. There is nothing to distract the visitor from the sight of scrubbed timber and creamy Bath Stone pillars set against whitewashed walls and ceiling; all serve to make this old church quite unforgettable. A leaflet and postcard are available at the church door.

On leaving the church, turn back towards the bridge and look out for a Footpath sign, where you bear sharp left to reach a kissing gate by which you enter a field. Follow the hedge on the left beside the Biss Brook until you reach a further kissing gate. These two gates are noteworthy – they were constructed locally from a redundant boiler and look as though they will survive well into the fourth millennium. After the second gate bear slightly right to leave the fields and reach the yard of Dilton Vale Farm.

Here turn left and very soon look out for a signposted path on your right. The entrance to this is by a low wooden gate which bears a small notice declaring, 'Landowners Welcome Caring Ramblers.' Follow the path through the grounds of the old brick house on your left until you reach a footbridge across the brook.

Here you bear right, across a tributary stream and stile, and head directly up the slope (the Greensand scarp), keeping to the right of a line of three trees. At the top you go through the squeeze-belly stile and follow the fence. Soon you are directed along a fenced footpath between fields, then beside a fence on your left.

When you reach the cross-track you turn left and then sharp right along a footpath which is sunk two or three feet below the fields on the right and the house gardens on the left. This eventually leads to a short flight of steps which drops you down onto a pavement beside the A350.

If you bear left towards the junction a hundred yards or so below you will find the Bell Inn at Chalford, should you require fortification for the final leg of the walk which is, be warned, mostly uphill.

Turn right and then left to leave the main road by Wellhead Drove (or left if you are leaving the pub). This lane leads past a few grand houses on the left, beside fields on the right, to woods ahead.

Take the left fork at the red-brick Westbury Waterworks pumping station; the beech wood and dell on your left mark the boundary between the Greensand and the Lower Chalk – the track ahead takes you onto the Lower Chalk – which again forms a terrace below the chalk scarp on your right.

If you scramble down into the dip directly opposite the Waterworks you will see the spring, or Wellhead.

After the Waterworks, the track ceases to be metalled but reverts to a green lane which follows a pleasant course below the scarp, whose crest you walked along in the first stage of this walk.

You eventually reach the road which leads from Westbury to the White Horse at a point marked by the White Horse Equestrian Centre. This sign is accompanied by one which read 'Slow Horses'; one wonders whether they also have bright horses. From this point the Westbury White Horse is clearly visible and is our target from here onwards.

Turn right at the road and continue climbing for almost half a mile. Look out for a sign on the left indicating a Public Footpath leading across fields towards the White Horse and the ramparts of Bratton Castle. Cross the stile here to enjoy the last stage of the walk. The right of way follows the edge of the steep escarpment towards the White Horse.

Once over a pair of stiles and out of the cultivated fields you will find a stone direction marker on the crest of the scarp. The height above sea level is 754 feet and, on a clear day, you can spend time finding all the landmarks indicated, and a few more besides. In the fields below, between the scarp and the cement works, crop circles may sometimes be seen.

Carry on until you reach the ramparts of Bratton Castle. The double bank and ditch of the Castle's southern perimeter are well preserved and of impressive proportions.

If you still have sufficient energy, it is worth scaling the fortifications to reach the enclosure which contains in its twenty-five acres a rather mutilated long barrow.

4 BUCKLAND DINHAM

via Orchardleigh, Spring Gardens and Elliots

Distance:	4.5 miles
Maps:	Pathfinders 1199, 1219; Explorer 155
	Landranger 183
Map Reference:	755513
Refreshment en route:	There are no opportunities en route but there is a pub, The Bell, in Buckland Dinham

THE WALK is an easy one through delightful country. There are field paths, tracks through woods, hills with distant views, ancient churches, streams and footbridges, and riverside meadows: an albeit unspectacular but nevertheless very appealing slice of rural Somerset. The only difficulty you may encounter is finding the route from Orchardleigh Church to the boundary of the estate but it's not impossible and don't let this put you off tackling the walk.

Buckland Dinham is an attractive village on a spur of land about three miles north-west of Frome. It was once a centre for the cloth trade. The church of St. Michael and All Angels is found a short distance uphill from the main road which passes through the village. Interesting features include an elaborate perpendicular tower and a doorway and two windows of the Norman period. Inside there is a Norman font, a Lady Chapel on the south side which has been restored this century and a north chapel which contains two effigies – a knight and his lady. These figures represent the donor Sir John Dinham, who died in 1332, and his wife. The original Dinham was Oliver de Dinant who held the manor in 1205 and hailed from Dinan in Britanny. Notice the old blind house just outside the church. (The author once had a close encounter in this church – see page 47).

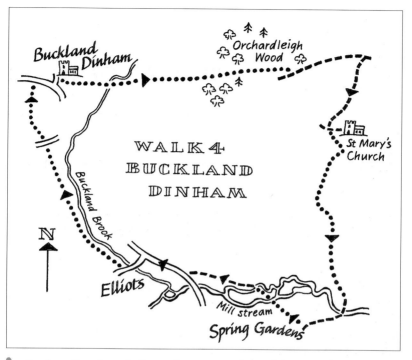

Facing the church from the approach road bear right along the signposted Public Footpath to Lullington. Follow the wall on the right until you reach a stile. Cross the stile to enter a field which slopes away towards Buckland Brook.

Walk down across the field to reach a wooden footbridge in the bottom left corner, then make for a steel-framed footbridge a little further on. Cross the next field diagonally towards a gate in the top left corner – if there is a standing crop it is advisable to follow the beaten path around the left hand boundary of this field to reach the same spot.

Leave this field and enter the next through the gate on the right. This field is narrow at this end – follow the hedgerow on your left and climb steadily, beside the hedge, until you reach a gap at the top left corner of the field to enter a wood.

Continue in the same direction along a roughly worn track through woods, passing a cottage away to the right. Carry on to reach the drive, the gate and cattle grid and the entrance to Orchardleigh Golf Club.

Follow the drive towards Orchardleigh House as far as some buildings on the right, where a track joins from the right. A sign here indicates 'Church'. Turn right here and follow the track down to the Church Lodge.

Follow the wall and fence on your left until the belfry of the church comes into view. You pass through two gates and cross a footbridge to reach the little island on which stands the tiny and ancient church of St. Mary.

Bear left and stroll round the church to see some of the gravestones. Those of the Duckworth family, until recently of Orchardleigh House, are grouped at the furthest extremity and look out over the lake, here almost entirely covered with a profusion of water lilies. Just behind them and lying under the yew tree are two small stones inscribed with the names of Henry Newbolt, Poet, and

his wife Margaret. On the wall of the porch is a new plate, dated 1989, referring to a nearby memorial.

The church itself consists only of nave, chancel, bellcote and north chapel. Notable features are the priest's door, piscina and aumbry and especially the various carved heads, including two either side of the sanctuary which formerly supported the Lenten veil (see page 39), and the stained glass.

The church survived the

Late 13th century piscina at Orchardleigh Church.

Reformation fairly intact and was sympathetically restored in 1879. Most of the carved heads and much of the stained glass is medieval and it is a fascinating exercise to view all these representations of the human face and pick out which are Victorian and which medieval. The difference of five or six centuries is quite striking and I leave it to the reader to make his own observations.

From the church gate turn left for a few yards until you can distinguish the stone marker situated on the rising slope to your right.

The fragment of shaped stone here marks the site of the old manor house which was demolished in 1856. The ground can be seen to be very uneven – a sure sign of vanished buildings.

Finding the route on from the marker needs full attention. Continue to climb uphill, ignoring all signs of beaten paths, but keeping a direct line from the church and the marker. You will eventually reach the end of the trees and will be confronted with an expanse of barren clay. This is spoil from the excavations to create the golf course which has rather ruined this ridge top locality.

Keep heading in the same direction, amid the clayey waste, until you reach a line of trees planted in line with the remains of a ha ha. This will lead you to a stile, marking the edge of the ridge, the boundary of Orchardleigh and the next stage of the walk.

First look back for a view of Orchardleigh House on the slope of the hill beyond and the lake below. In other directions can be seen – to the east the Westbury White Horse, to the south Cley Hill, then the wooded hills of Longleat with the town of Frome in the foreground.

Cross the stile and bear left to follow a rough but well-marked path downhill, through trees and into a field; now follow the field boundary on your left. Cross a stile and follow the track along the edge of a field, then beside some trees until you reach a gate beyond which is a stone bridge.

Follow the lane ahead to a number of bridges. The restored and converted Spring Gardens Mill can be seen away to your right. Simply carry on along the lane ahead for a couple of hundred yards.

You leave the lane towards the first house on the right – Jeffries Mill. Turn left over a stile beside a gate, then a second stile, then a step stile to reach a drive. Cross the drive and continue in a straight line towards the tree-lined stream beyond.

About twenty yards to the left of the sluice gate through which you will hear water rushing there is a stone footbridge, not always obvious in the undergrowth. Cross this bridge, climb the stile on the far side and head across the field towards another footbridge to the left of the farm buildings. Now bear left along the drive from Brookover Farm to the main road. You reach the main road at a point where an entrance gateway to the Orchardleigh Estate is flanked by lodges.

Bear right up the main road for a short distance (walk in single file if you are one of a party) before turning left down a minor road through the hamlet known as Elliots. Once past the buildings look out for a stone stile on the right under a massive beech tree. Leave the lane here and head down across the field towards a wooden stile opposite.

You now follow a pleasant field path beside Buckland Brook towards Buckland Dinham, where the church tower soon hoves into view. There are various field crossings to negotiate; the right of way is visibly beaten all the way – keep the brook on your right and you won't go wrong.

As you enter the last field before the houses on the lower slope of the field ahead, make for the gap between the houses. Here you will find a large stone stile which drops you into a lane. The field path continues directly opposite. In this field, head for a stile in the top left corner, then follow the hedgerow on the right, and cross two more stiles and a kissing gate before reaching houses. Simply continue in the same direction until you reach the main road through the village. At the main road bear right and then first left to reach the main road through the village. Turn left for the Bell pub and right for the church.

Orchardleigh had a poet attached to it when Henry Newbolt married one of the Duckworths. In his poem 'Fidele's Grassy Tomb', Newbolt relates the story of the squire of Orchardleigh who, on his death bed, asked for his dog Fidele, who had once saved his life, to be buried at his feet in the family chapel. This was done, but when the Bishop of Bath and Wells heard that a dog had been buried in church he ordered that the parson remove Fidele to the churchyard beside the lake. The sexton was given instructions but could not bring himself to disturb Fidele. In the words of Henry Newbolt:

> *The grave was dug; the mason came*
> *And carved on stone Fidele's name;*
> *But the dog that the Sexton laid inside*
> *Was a dog that never had lived or died.*
>
> *So the Parson was praised, and the scandal stayed,*
> *Till, a long time after, the church decayed,*
> *And, laying the floor anew, they found*
> *In the tomb of the Squire the bones of a hound.*

ORCHARDLEIGH

5 CLAVERTON

via Bathampton Down & the Kennet and Avon Canal

Distance:	5.5 miles
Maps:	Pathfinder 1183; Explorer 155
	Landranger 172
Map Reference:	788642
Refreshment en route:	The Hope and Anchor is at Midford, the half-way point.

THE WALK is an exhilarating one which includes a trek around Bathampton Down with its magnificent views over Bath and the hills beyond – Lansdown, Little Solsbury Hill, Charmy Down, Banner Down and Bathford Hill. All these hills are essentially composed of the near horizontal strata of Oolitic Limestone, or Bath Stone, once much worked in this locality as a source of excellent building stone. Indeed, there are many signs of quarrying activity to be seen in the perambulation of Bathampton Down.

The ascent of Bathampton Down is by lane from Claverton and entails a steady climb over about half a mile; the descent to the Kennet and Avon Canal is considerably steeper.

There are no pubs anywhere on this walk but Bathampton Down provides a choice of picnic sites, so long as you are careful not to obstruct the golf course.

Claverton (the name means the farm where burdock grows) is a linear village on the lower slopes of Bathampton Down arranged along a street which runs parallel to the main road a short distance below. In the centre are some attractive terraces enclosed by stone walls; these are all that remain of the old manor house, which dated from the late sixteenth century. The house was rebuilt in the early eighteenth century much higher up the hill with commanding views

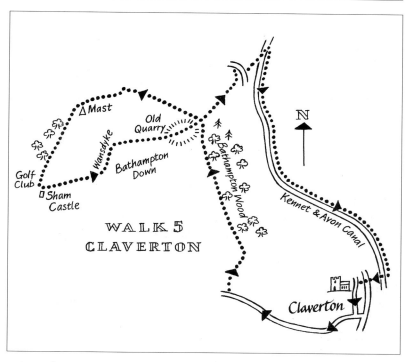

across the valley of the River Avon. Claverton Manor now houses the American Museum, so that the public has access to the house and grounds.

St. Mary's Church may be reached by a footpath from the street through the village. The church was heavily restored in the mid-nineteenth century and is unusual in that the chancel seems to be as long as the nave. The church contains a striking monument to Sir William Basset (died 1613) and his wife. This is in the form of life-size sculptures of the couple brightly painted and set upright in niches in the side of the chancel. Outside there is a good example of a scratch dial on the porch and, in the churchyard, Ralph Allen's mausoleum crowned with a great stone pyramid. Ralph Allen was a great friend of Richard Graves who was rector of Claverton for fifty-five years. In the churchyard also are the graves of four of Cromwell's soldiers who were killed in action in 1643, Claverton Manor having been captured by the Parliamentary General, Sir William Waller.

With your back to the church bear right past some houses until you reach the lane. Turn right here and begin the ascent of Bathampton Down. The lane swings first to the left, then to the right: the woods on the right are in the grounds of Claverton Manor, the valley below to the left forms a steep and narrow cleft in the Down in which Vineyard Farm is situated.

You pass the entrance to Claverton Manor (the American Museum) and, when the lane begins to level out, you pass a signposted Private Car Park which belongs to the Museum. A few yards past the entrance to the car park, in the stone wall on the right, there is a stile in the form of projecting stone steps.

Climb the wall here and bear slightly to the right to follow the field boundary on the right. As you cross another attractive stile (illustrated above), you will see a signpost in the field beyond indicating that this piece of land is known as Bushey Norwood, and belongs to the National Trust. Bath University is the unlovely sprawl of buildings away to the left.

The right of way follows the field boundary on the right-hand side towards a kissing gate in the far right-hand corner about half a mile beyond.

You may be intrigued by the many large stones scattered around the field, some of which are set on end in a rather unnatural way. Bathampton Down, like Little Solsbury Hill, a little to the north, was used by the natives before Roman times for cultivation and settlement. These upright stones are mere stones which were erected to define field boundaries (see illustration page 45).

Once through the kissing gate keep to the main path through the wood which bears a little to the right and gradually loses height.

You are somewhat below the summit of the down; there is higher ground to the left and the hillside falls away steeply to the right. There is much evidence of former quarrying activity in the shape of numerous mounds and hollows.

To follow the right of way you should simply stick to the most well used path. The woods become thicker until you reach a crosstrack. There is a rudimentary steel stile opposite and just below this point. Do not cross here but turn left up the hill. After a short distance the path emerges into the open: here you immediately turn sharp right towards a stile.

Cross the stile and head straight on towards the trees — simply follow the beaten path until you emerge into the open on the slopes of Bathampton Down which face north towards Batheaston. You now follow the right of way in the same direction you took through the woods, i.e. towards Bath or, more immediately, towards the trees on the far side of this open field.

You now make your way ahead, with the trees on your right and the mast to your left. Notice a number of tumuli in the hillside to your left. Continue to follow the edge of the woods on your right towards a stile and kissing gate to the right and past the buildings belonging to Bath Golf Club until you reach the Sham Castle.

Sham Castle, an artificial ruin, was built by Ralph Allen, to beautify the view from his townhouse in North Parade in Bath, Prior Park having not yet been built. It is perhaps surprising that anyone should want to build an artificial ruin, but perhaps even more surprising that the eighteenth-century love of order should demand that the Sham Castle's façade be absolutely symmetrical. But whoever heard of a symmetrical ruin?

To continue the walk: from the Castle retrace your steps to the Golf Club's car park. Turn right to follow the track beside the hedgerow, ascending gently. The track forks and levels out as it reaches a clump of trees on the right. The right fork is signposted as a permissive path; the left forks as a Public Footpath. Take the left fork and cross the fairway of the golf course towards a gap in the low ridge ahead. Pass through the gap and follow the embankment on the left.

Bathampton Down was certainly the site of a pre-Roman settlement as the tumuli and evidence of Iron Age agriculture testify. It is likely that the linear earthwork here was built to protect the original Iron Age enclosure. Some authorities refer to the earthwork as part of the post-Roman Wansdyke and its form – a simple ditch and north-facing bank – and its position in relation to the east and west sections of the Wansdyke, would seem to support this view. (for Notes on the Wansdyke, see page 55).

Follow the embankment as far as a T-junction marked by a pair of Public Footpath signs indicating Bathampton Down to the left. Head straight on, by the fifteenth tee, to reach the edge of a former quarry. This is not a dangerous site, however, as there is no sheer drop to the bottom level. By following the edge a few yards to the right you will find a gentle path to the base of the quarry.

Before moving on from this high point it is worth taking a final view of the landscape. There is a panorama stretching from the Georgian terraces of Bath strung along and stacked upon the slopes of Lansdown in the west, to Brown's Folly standing above the dense woods of Bathford Hill to the east. Between these there is the

Mere stones, Bushey Norwood

limestone plateau of this southern fringe of the Cotswolds disected into isolated masses by rivers and streams, including the River Avon, Lam Brook, St. Catherine's Brook and By Brook. The Fosse Way runs straight from Bath north-eastwards to Batheaston and is then forced to stray from its direct course in order to ascend Banner Down on whose summit it resumes its characteristic straight course, but now in a more northerly direction, in order to avoid meeting the steep-sided valley of the By Brook.

The Celtic field system of Bathampton Down can be seen well from this point too. Looking down on the north-facing slope, the outlines of small rectangular fields are visible although the laying out of a golf course with greens and bunkers and trees has not helped.

From the bottom of the quarry walk along the excavated hollow towards the exit where you begin to descend by the steep, straight track which you earlier partly ascended; you now follow this track to the main road far below.

You may notice some large blocks of stone marked with deep grooves embedded in this track. These are most likely the old stone sleeper blocks in which the iron rails of the tramway serving the quarry were set. This inclined plane system consisted of two lines – one by which loaded wagons descended by a rope and another by which empty wagons ascended.

At the main road, cross over with care and turn right. As the bend straightens out look for a public footpath on the left – here cross the stile and continue down to the footbridge across the canal. Cross over and turn right along the towpath which you follow for about one and a half miles to Claverton. Cross the second bridge below the village and follow the lane – look out for a stile on the right which affords a short cut to the main road and thence via a kissing gate to the village street below the church.

Close Encounter at Buckland Dinham (Walk 4)

The first occasion I visited the church at Buckland Dinham I had a strange experience. It was a gloomy Sunday afternoon when I entered the church. As the door slammed shut behind me I stepped into the nave and immediately sensed there was someone else in the church. I instinctively looked towards the chancel and saw a figure – an old, wizened man dressed in black and holding a Bible. He stood beside the choir stalls and stared intently at me.

He seemed neither hostile nor friendly but looked at me as though I had interrupted him. I was somewhat taken aback and looked away for a moment. When I looked back he was gone and I realised I had seen a ghost (and I am certainly not one given to seeing ghosts).

I have visited the church subsequently (having asked for the key in a nearby cottage) but have not run in to the aged cleric again. My only explanation for what happened is that I had disturbed the ghost of some former incumbent carrying out his Christian duties on a Sunday when the Church was empty.

6 CLEY HILL

via Corsley Heath and the Whitbournes

Distance:	Five miles
Maps:	Pathfinder 1220
	Landranger 183
Map Reference:	838444
Refreshment en route:	Royal Oak pub at Corsley Heath, about two-thirds of the way.

THE WALK includes a number of field paths, tracks and lanes. Just inside Wiltshire, the country traversed has a definite Wiltshire feel about it, with spacious fields and wide open vistas on the slopes of Cley Hill, though some writers note that the isolated knoll of Cley Hill puts them in mind of Somerset and the similarly abrupt and solitary hills which occur in and around the low-lying Sedgemoor.

You descend from the chalk of Cley Hill to the Greensand at Corsley Heath and the wooded hills of Longleat. There is a nasty road crossing on the very last leg of the walk.

Cley Hill is National Trust property and can be approached from the A362 – the Warminster-Frome road – a car park is provided a short distance from the main road. The view from the summit is well worth the climb.

To begin the walk: carry on by the track from the small car park towards the hill. Soon you reach a barn on the right. Take the deeply sunken lane to your right. Follow this old way until the path forks – ignore the somewhat more overgrown path ahead but bear left towards a stile by a corrugated iron shed to reach the field on the left. Cley Hill is straight ahead at this point.

The right of way now continues along the edge of this field, following the hedgerow on your right. Cross the step stile into the

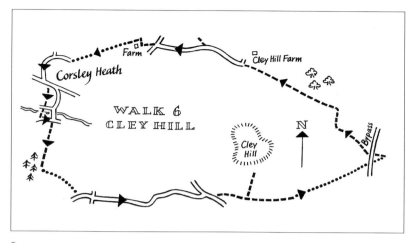

next field and again follow the hedgerow on your right, through a steel gate by the beaten path towards the Warminster bypass.

In the distance ahead you can see the wooded eminence of Arn Hill above the town. Make for the double wooden step stile beside the trough near the corner of the field; cross the stile and turn left along the concrete farm track.

There is a signpost near the tunnel beneath the bypass, indicating the direction to Warminster and Longleat. Our way is not indicated. We need to bear left by the concrete track and through the gate. Soon the concrete gives way to a grassy track. Carry on following the barbed wire fence in the same direction.

When the fence ends you bear right towards the corner of the field, then left along the beaten track, soon following a course between hedgebanks. When the track stops, continue in the same direction by following the narrow footpath which meanders through the undergrowth.

You reach a steel gate where you can look down to Cley Hill Farm and beyond to the elongated, ridge-top village of Chapmanslade. Keep the fence on your left and head downhill until you reach the steel gate; go through here to reach another gate; and continue by the sunken lane opposite. Bear left when you reach the metalled lane. Eventually you reach a junction. Cross over and follow the lane on the far side.

Corsley Church and Cley Hill

Carry on along the lane, past two pairs of semi-detached houses on the right, until you reach a junction. Go straight across here along the drive to Park Farm House.

Turn right at the house and follow the boundary wall until you reach a stile at the point where it ends. Turn left here to cross the stile; now follow the track ahead in a straight line, via a couple of crossings, towards the buildings of Corsley Heath. As you approach the houses, follow the right of way as it curves leftwards to climb the slope a little and reach the exit from the field on your right.

Follow the lane to reach the T-junction ahead; turn left until you reach the main road. Across the road from here is the Royal Oak pub. Cross the road and bear left; look out for a stile just before Corsley Post Office. Cross the stile and soon another. Now follow the hedge on the left and descend the field to cross a couple of stiles and follow the hedgerow on the left to reach the bottom left corner. Turn right at the lane and then sharp left down a metalled footpath between cottages.

Do not go through the gate to the left but bear slightly to the right along the path between hedges. Cross the stream at the bottom and then follow the narrow way uphill to reach a stile – now head for the gate on the lane.

Turn left and then right at the junction ahead, up the concrete track. This soon leads to a green way between hedges. Carry on until the way levels out and you find a stile in the fence on the left. Cross here and head across the top of this field to reach a stile in the far corner, to the right of a plantation of conifers. Now follow the plantation to your left. Cross the stile ahead to enter a large open field. The right of way once followed a field boundary here which is now vanished. Carry on in the same general direction but slightly to the right by the beaten path to reach a wooden stile in the barbed wire fence.

Turn left on reaching the lane, then straight across at the junction below – note an entrance to Longleat to the right. This is a pleasant lane with little traffic and good views towards Cley Hill. Continue by the No Entry Sign to reach the main road.

Cross the road here but TAKE GREAT CARE. The view in either direction is fairly restricted; use your eyes and ears to sense approaching vehicles and cross over when it is all clear (if there are several of you together, make sure you all cross at the same time). PLEASE NOTE: You can increase the visibility a little, particularly to the left, by crossing to the left of the grass triangle at the junction.

After only 50 yards or so you will reach the entrance to a sunken way on the left. Make your way along here until you reach the hay barn near the car park and the starting point of the walk.

7 COMBE HAY

via Odd Down and Southstoke

Distance:	4 miles
Maps:	Pathfinders 1183,1199; Explorer 155
	Landranger 172
Map Reference:	735598
Refreshment en route:	The Wheatsheaf at Combe Hay;
	The Packhorse at Southstoke

THE WALK comprises an easy half day's ramble. The route includes lanes, tracks, field paths, the Wansdyke and sight of the Fosse Way.

Combe Hay is a straggling village built on a south facing slope which looks down towards Cam Brook. The village church, which has a small perpendicular tower, is at the southern end of the village, rather hidden behind the trees of the churchyard and close by Combe Hay Manor. If you venture beyond the semi-circular apse at the east end of the church you can see, over the church wall, the east façade of the manor house. The house is eighteenth century, partly c. 1730 and partly c. 1770. The east façade, in sight here, is strictly classical, and very restrained. The Bath Stone used is particularly honey-coloured and is most attractive in the morning sun. The church is fairly undistinguished, having been much restored in the last century. Notice the stables which face the church across the churchyard; these Pevsner dates at c. 1700.

With your back to the church turn left up the hill. At the crossroads bear right along the lane signposted to Bath.

Notice the wall of engineering bricks immediately on the right. This forms the head of a tunnel of the old, disused Camerton branch

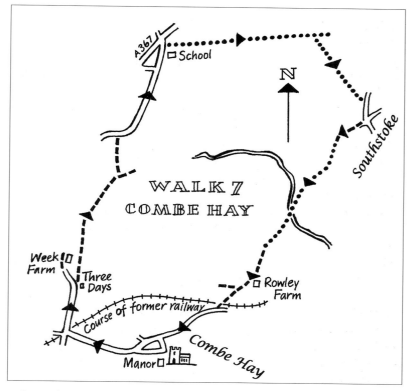

railway line. If you look over the wall you can see the cutting; the line was tunnelled under the road junction at this point. The house to the left is named 'Tunnel Farm House'.

Ignore a public footpath sign on the left but at the fork ahead bear right and pass the cottage named 'Three Days'. The considerable range of derelict buildings on the slope to your left is Week Farm. A little farther on you pass Fortnight Farm to your left. Keep following the track uphill to a point where it swings to the right where there is a gate and stile which lead into a sloping field. Cross the stile and climb up to the telegraph pole directly ahead. Once you reach this feature simply carry on in the same direction until you arrive at an old five-bar gate at the field edge. Leg it over this.

Before you continue onwards by the track through the woods, do rest at the gate and look back to enjoy the splendid view down the cleft in which Fortnight and Week Farms are situated. Beyond them is the valley of Cam Brook and, beyond it, the ridge which separates the Cam and Wellow Brooks.

Week Farm, Combe Hay

At the junction of tracks and lanes above, walk straight on along the metalled road towards Odd Down. The long, low stone wall to your left has been made good and now forms the perimeter of a large car park which services the Bath Park and Ride scheme. Ahead are the roof-tops of Bath's southern fringe. You cross a road which leads to a new housing estate fancifully named 'Sulis Meadows'. Walk past St. Gregory's School and look out for an iron gate and squeezer stile on the right.

Before passing through the stile notice the name of the road which crosses at the junction ahead: 'The Old Fosse Road'. The modern road here follows the course of the Roman road before it descends to the ancient spa.

Once through the stile you follow the level path flanked by houses, playing fields and agricultural fields. You are now traversing the plateau-like summit of Odd Down.

This path is along the Wansdyke, which in parts can be seen to be a good ten feet above the level of the land to the north. The Wansdyke is a linear earthwork and occurs in two distinct parts, the East and West Wansdyke . The East Wansdyke is certainly the more spectacular and traverses the Marlborough Downs whilst the West Wansdyke runs in an east-west alignment south of Bristol and Bath, of which this section across Odd Down is a part. The Wansdyke consists of a single bank with a ditch on the northern side, thereby implying that it was built by a people living on the south side in defence against an enemy to the north. It is probable, therefore, that it was built by the Britons, under the command of Ambrosius and his lieutenant Arthur, against the Saxons.

Past the school playing fields has risen the new housing estate of Sulis Meadows. 1,400 years ago, roughly, Britons glared at Saxons across the Berlin Wall of the Wansdyke; now the once mighty earthwork cowers beneath the onward march of bland suburbia.

Continue along the footpath until you reach a stone wall on your right which marks a field boundary. Bear right here and follow the stone wall towards the trees ahead. Leaving the field, you cross a concreted track and pass through a fine old iron kissing gate. Carry on through the trees, across a drive, until the path drops down to reach a lane. Bear right here and follow the lane into Southstoke.

The little village green, marked by white railings and a bench seat, is a good spot to rest before the last leg of the walk back to Combe Hay. Alternatively, you may seek refreshment at the Packhorse pub, which is by the road below the green. This interesting and unspoilt pub has a seventeenth century, three-gabled façade and an unspoilt interior which is worth seeing. They serve a good pint and offer very reasonably priced bar food.

From the green (facing the church) bear right, past the church, farm and barn. Carry on through the gap beside the gate, heading downhill. A little way down, as the lane bends to the left, there is an iron squeezer stile on the right. Pass through and follow the beaten path downhill, past the recently restored house on your left (now holiday cottages), to a large ash tree which marks the left corner of the wooded area below. From here follow the well-worn footpath downhill, keeping the wood on your right.

As you descend here you can look ahead to see the continuation of this footpath as it ascends the hill opposite – this is our route. Continue to descend until you reach the stream at the bottom, which seems to keep flowing in even the driest conditions. Cross over by the stepping stones and cross the stile on the far side to reach the path which climbs uphill – the right of way here is signposted as part of the 'Limestone Link'. In winter you can pinpoint the wooden step stile at the summit though it is more difficult to see in summer.

Climb this bosky slope until you reach the stile. Cross into a field and follow the beaten track beside the hedgebank to your right. You will see the roof-tops of Rowley Farm a little beyond. Look out for a stile on your right; climb over and bear left to follow the hedge to a track which leads you past the buildings of Rowley Farm. Beyond the farmhouse you will see the tower of Combe Hay church directly ahead. Follow the track downhill until you reach the lane – notice the entrance drive to Caisson House on the left.

It was here that the famous caisson lock was built on the Somerset Coal Canal. Directly opposite this drive you can see a short stretch of the canal, now dry, but unmistakable nevertheless. Just before you reach the road, you will pass by a brick wall like the one at Tunnel Farm House (at the start of the walk). This marks another railway tunnel – a peer over the top will reveal the old cutting.

Bear right at the lane and gradually descend into the village. If you would like to visit the Wheatsheaf pub – and it is a delight with its large garden – you should keep your eyes skinned for a signboard on the right; the pub is elevated above the lane and is easily missed.

Nunney Castle and moat, north side (Walk 12)

8 DUNDAS AQUEDUCT

via Conkwell, Farleigh Wick and River Avon

Distance:	4 miles
Maps:	Pathfinders 1183, 1184; Explorer 155
	Landrangers 172,173
Map Reference:	784627
Refreshment en route:	The Fox and Hounds pub is at Farleigh Wick, the half-way point.

THE WALK is almost entirely by field paths and green tracks and includes a lovely stretch of the River Avon and Limpley Stoke valley. This is a quiet and peaceful walk through meadows and woods and across hillsides with magnificent views.

There is adequate parking near the Dundas Aqueduct in a lay-by beside the A361 about a quarter of a mile beyond the Viaduct Inn on the right as you drive towards Claverton, or on the left just before the BP garage as you approach from Bath. The canal can be reached from either end of the lay-by: a footpath leads down from the Claverton end and a track from the other end.

The wide basin here marks the junction of the Kennet and Avon Canal, now fully restored, and the former Somerset Coal Canal, which here began its course towards the Somerset Coalfield, and has itself been restored for about a quarter of a mile from its junction with the K & A to provide mooring facilities for the growing number of craft now using the canal.

Cross the canal by the bridge beyond the old crane, then cross the aqueduct, a rather magnificent three-arched bridge which here carries the canal across both the railway and the river.

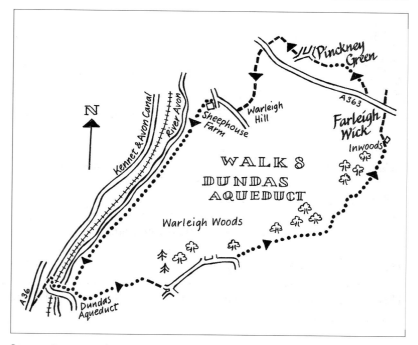

Once you have reached the far bank, keep walking straight ahead, to the left of the single-storey workshop and across a stile marked 'Public Path'. Immediately past the woodland to your left you leave the sunken way by climbing up to a gap on your left where you enter a sloping field. Head obliquely up and across the field to the top left corner where you reach a stile beside a water trough. Continue in the same direction, with the wood to your right, towards the top left corner. Here you continue uphill by a stony, sunken path.

You emerge at the hamlet of Conkwell at the bottom of its single street at Spring Cottage; the spring can be seen in the hillside in front of the cottage. Other houses also tell a story in their names: there is Cromwell's Rest, where Oliver Cromwell is said to have rested between military engagements (it is also said that his men poisoned all the wells in the vicinity except that at Conkwell), and Old Bounds Cottage, which marks the Somerset-Wiltshire boundary.

Looking back at Conkwell from the top of its one steep street puts one in mind of a Cornish fishing village where the cottages are stacked steeply in a narrow cleft leading down to the sea.

Crane and canal basin at Dundas Aqueduct

Turn left at the top of the village and straight on at the T-junction ahead. Shortly past the junction, look out for a stone stile on the left which leads into a field and to a footpath beside an enclosed wood, which you continue to follow through three fields.

At the end of the third field, where the fenced way follows the field boundary to the right, bear left through the gate and keep the wood on your left, then a little to the right at the field boundary ahead. Now go through the gate into a field which is all but surrounded by woods. Follow the right hand boundary until you reach a gate on the right. Make for this gap through the woods until you emerge into a field. Now turn left and follow the woods on your left.

Look out for a wooden stile beside a gate on the left, back into the woods. Follow the track through the woods and once more emerge into a field. Now follow the boundary wall of Inwoods House on your left. Carry on past the house and turn left through a gate which leads into a kind of yard surrounded by various outbuildings. Keep bearing right and follow the drive until you reach the main road.

Turn left, past the Fox and Hounds pub and Midway Cottage. Cross the road with care and look for the Public Footpath signpost opposite. This leads to steps down to a sunken way towards the hamlet of Farleigh Wick. Follow this sunken way until you reach a point where a tree has fallen across the path. Bear right here – look for the yellow arrow on the tree trunk and climb up the bank to reach a pair of stiles on the left. Now head towards the buildings and make your way to the driveway which gives access to them; follow this drive and bear left at the grassy triangle ahead.

Cross the lane and enter the drive to Douch Farm Nurseries, but continue in the same direction by the enclosed path which skirts the boundary of Douch Farm to the right.

Follow this right of way until it takes you left and down to the Dry Arch under the main road. Carry on by the main path through the woods ahead (not over the stone stile on the right). Simply follow the track through the woods, taking a right fork (note the improvised blue arrow) where the path bifurcates – you will enjoy glimpses over the valley towards Claverton – and press on until the path drops you into the lane which runs between Conkwell and Warleigh.

Turn right and follow the lane until you reach Sheephouse Farm on the left. Turn sharp left, along the drive towards the farm, past the various outbuildings, then follow the arrows by bearing right along a fenced, permissive path. This leads you to a couple of stiles – follow the beaten path down towards the river and all the way upstream towards Dundas Aqueduct, which can be seen ahead.

Head towards the stile at the rear of the boathouse beneath the aqueduct and make your way up the steps to reach the canal towpath. From here you retrace your steps across the aqueduct, across the canal by the footbridge and up to the lay-by on the main road.

9 HOLT

via Great Chalfield and Little Chalfield

Distance:	Four miles
Maps:	Pathfinder 1184; Explorer 155
	Landranger 173
Map Reference:	859617
Refreshment en route:	The Toll Gate and The Old Ham Tree in Holt

THE WALK is an easy one, using well-trodden paths, with no steep slopes. The route includes the magnificent medieval manor house of Great Chalfield.

The most attractive part of Holt is at its western end around the village green, or Ham Green as it is known on account of its ham-like shape. It is usually possible to find somewhere to park around the green so this acts as the starting point for the walk.

- *Take the minor road which leads away from Ham Green towards the south-east. This way is soon signposted, interestingly, as 'Gaston (leading to Star)'. You soon reach the Parish Church of St. Katherine.*

The church, with the exception of the tower and entrance to the south porch, was entirely rebuilt in 1891, but in medieval Gothic style.

- *Bear left, past the church, by a track which leads to a kissing gate and a footpath through a field.*

The grounds of The Courts are on the left. The seven acres of gardens are owned by the National Trust and are open to the public in the summer months although the house, which has an elegant eighteenth century façade, is not.

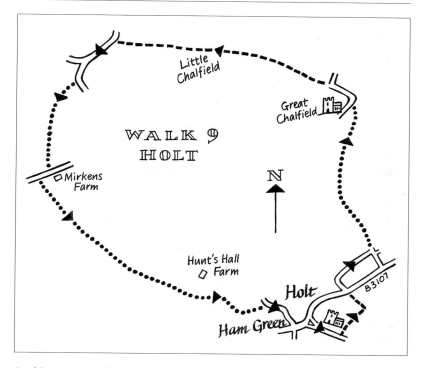

• *You approach a pair of squeezer stiles: one ahead and another to*
• *your left. Take the latter and follow the track to reach the main road*
• *through the village at the entrance to The Courts.*

Before crossing the road notice the United Reformed Church
buildings on the left: the older, plainer structure behind, with its
pointed windows and hipped roof dates from 1810.

• *Cross the road, pass Holt Village Hall (ex Holt Reading Rooms 1873,*
• *according to the inscribed stone tablet in the wall), and walk along*
• *the road called 'The Midlands'. Bear right at Beaven's Leather Works*
• *(established 1770) and walk past a number of mainly industrial*
• *buildings of brick and stone.*

Look out for a surprise: beneath a wall at right angles to the road is an old
pump set into the bricked-up entrance to a former well-house. The entrance

*Pump at
Holt Spa*

is framed by a pair of Tuscan columns surmounted by a straight entablature. Below the stone is the following inscription: 'Sacred to the memory of Lady Lisle and the Revd. James Lewis, the persons who patronised this spring and rendered it famous in the year 1720.' This pump marks the site of a former spa which once rivalled Bath.

Once past factory buildings bear left along a track to enter a field by a stile. Continue straight ahead, ignoring the gate on the right. Instead, head to the left of this gate and walk on between hedgebanks as the field narrows. Cross the stile beside the gate and head up and across the next field, bearing very slightly to the right until you reach a stile in the hedgebank at the top which leads you into the next field. Follow the hedgebank on the right a short distance and cross the next stile. Great Chalfield and Mill Cottages are now visible across the field to the left.

Cross the brook below by a wooden bridge and head across the field to find the exit into the lane at the top left-hand corner, just above Mill Cottages. Follow the lane beside the moat and fortified boundary wall of Great Chalfield, past the diminutive All Saints Church and magnificent manor house, which belongs to the National Trust and is open to the public in the summer.

There is so much worth seeing in this late medieval manor house, in the church and the grounds, that it would be futile to attempt a full description here – a visit is recommended.

Continue to walk in the same direction along the track past Great Chalfield towards Little Chalfield. Walk on along an avenue and bear left at the lane ahead. Once over the stream in the valley bottom, look for the Public Footpath sign on the right – ascend the right of way beside the hedgerow on your left.

At the top you cross a stile into the next field and continue in the same general direction until you reach a lane opposite Merkins Farm. Turn right here and then left just past the first house you reach. Follow this track as it leads you into a field which offers a wide view south across the Clay Vale towards the escarpment of Salisbury Plain.

Walk straight on with the hedge on your left, and then, when the hedge takes a turn to the left, head in the same direction to reach a stile in the far field boundary. Follow the same direction again in the next field until you reach a further stile in the bottom left corner. Now head for the next two stiles, the latter leading you immediately to a further crossing to the left. Cross here and follow the hedgerow on your right, beneath the pylon.

There is a group of farm buildings – Hunt's Hall Farm – across the field to your left. Head straight on to reach a stile in the hedgerow about twenty yards or so to the left of this field's right hand corner.

Now head diagonally across the next field, towards Holt, through a broken hedgerow, to the field's top left corner. Turn sharp left here and cross the stile immediately to hand in the corner. Now follow the beaten path towards the buildings of Holt village. There are two exits: the one leftward is by a kissing gate which drops you onto the lane at the very edge of the village. The one rightwards leads you between houses to reach the lane. In both cases you turn right to return to Ham Green.

10 LIMPLEY STOKE

via Midford, Pipehouse and Hinton Priory

Distance:	4.5 miles
Maps:	Pathfinders 1183, 1199; Explorer 155
	Landranger 172
Map Reference:	783603
Refreshment en route:	The Hope and Anchor pub is at Midford, the half-way point.

The walk provides a variety of scenery and much of interest. There is a long descent from Limpley Stoke to the Midford Brook and a gentler ascent from Midford to Pipehouse Lane.

- *The starting point for this walk is Limpley Stoke parish church.*
- *The lane outside the church is too narrow for parking a car; it may*
- *be possible to find space in the road opposite the church or a little*
- *further along (northwards), the lane widens sufficiently to allow*
- *parking.*

St. Mary's Church is set high on a hill on the southern edge of Limpley Stoke, and stands aloof from the village centre. Limpley Stoke is built at various levels on the north-facing hillside: there is Lower Stoke, Middle Stoke and Upper Stoke, where the church is situated. The various levels are connected by a number of painfully vertical footpaths – notice the one opposite the church which is heralded by a handsome old stone squeezer stile and a badly chipped but antique enamel notice.

St. Mary's is an ancient church, as the Saxon arch (once a doorway) in the arcade testifies. We are told that behind the oak panelling in the chancel are to be found Roman tiles laid in a herring-bone pattern, the tiles having been taken from a Roman settlement sited nearby.

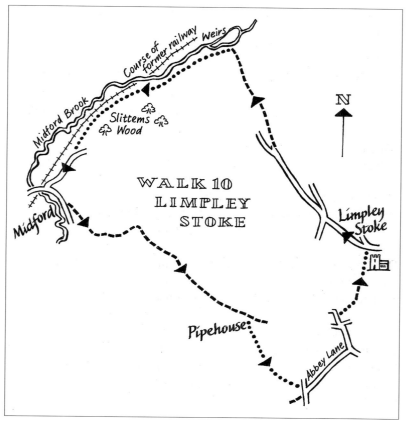

We are also told that the nave walls are believed to be those of a small chapel built in 1001 to mark the boundary of land given by Ethelred, son of King Edgar, to the Abbess of Shaftesbury in 973. Shaftesbury Abbey became the richest Abbey in England and was given the Manor of Bradford in 1001. The boundary between Somerset and Wiltshire, as well as that between the parishes of Limpley Stoke (in Wiltshire) and Freshford (in Somerset), passes through the field immediately behind the church.

St. Mary's is a small, simple and unrestored church. It has a low, plain, unbuttressed tower surmounted by a short spire, partly hidden behind a parapet. The porch is early thirteenth century with a round-headed arch and a statue of the madonna and child looking out of a

niche above the door. Inside, in addition to the plain and narrow
Saxon arch, there is a fine stone pulpit built into the north wall,
Jacobean panelling on the balcony of the gallery and a font whose
bowl is believed to be of Saxon origin. No list of the church's fabric
can really convey the peace and charm of this ancient place of
worship – do take time to soak in the atmosphere, it will do you
good.

St. Mary's Church, Limpley Stoke

*With your back to the church, turn left along Church Lane, cross
the Warminster Road (with care!) and continue along Midford Lane
on the far side. Go straight on, past the stone mine, until you reach
a forked turning where you bear right along a lane signposted 'Old
Track'. Quite soon there is a right-hand turning which leads towards
more houses. Ignore this but go straight ahead by the unmetalled
track, to the left of a bungalow named 'Chatleys'.*

*The track begins to descend, at first gently, then more steeply.
At the cross track below turn right, then sharp left, and continue to
descend to the valley bottom. There are some good views from here
towards Monkton Combe and the course of the old Camerton Branch
Railway can be traced where it cuts into the opposite slope.*

As you reach the river you will see the old mill buildings straight ahead; these can be reached by a footpath which crosses the island lying between Midford Brook and the mill stream. However, to contiune the walk you bear left over the stile before the footbridge and follow the riverside footpath. You soon pass a dilapidated weir.

Follow the river for about half a mile. Eventually the footpath forsakes the river at a point where the course of the old railway crossed the Midford Brook by a bridge. The path rises at this point – keep the wood on your left and the railway embankment on your right. Head forward to reach a stile, then another, then a gap in a stone wall.

You will pass a cutting through the embankment which provides a view north-westwards towards Tucking Mill. However, there is no right of way through the cutting: continue the walk by following the beaten path with the embankment on your right.

Notice Midford Castle on the crest of the hill opposite. This unique complex of buildings dates from the late eighteenth century; the group includes a gatehouse, stables, chapel and summer house, while the main house is in the form of a triangle, with circular towers at each corner. According to an old guide book, the reason for this curious plan is as follows: 'A well known society gambler once made a fortune at the card tables by turning up the ace of clubs; in the hopes of perpetuating his good luck, he built this residence.' (*By the By-Ways Around Bristol*, 1927)

Again, simply follow the beaten path until you reach a gate by which you join the lane from Limpley Stoke to Midford; here bear right down to the main road.

The walk contiunes from here by turning left. However, you may be ready for a spot of refreshment – the Hope and Anchor is easily reached by turning right. Even if you don't wish to visit the pub, it is worth pausing here to take in the scene. Immediately on the right are the remains of the bridge which carried the Radstock branch line across the main road. A little further is the road bridge across Midford Brook, and, just beyond the Hope and Anchor, the bridge which carried the Somerset and Dorset. Imagine what a busy spot Midford must have been in the heyday of steam!

Back at Midford Lane, turn left and look out for the beginning of an unmetalled track, indicated as a Byway, a hundred yards or so on the left. Follow this old sunken way uphill for about a mile.

Soon after the track levels out you reach houses at the hamlet of Pipehouse. Keep your eyes peeled for the former 'Village Room 1903' (according to a tablet set in the wall) on the left. Directly opposite there is a stile and footpath leading away from the lane on the right. Follow this hedge until you reach a stile, then a number of gates/stiles to enter an open field.

Head across this field to reach a stile just to the right of a solitary tree. Climb over and continue in a half-left direction towards the gatehouse at Hinton Priory. You leave the field by a stile beside a gate to reach the main road, A36.

It is possible to gain some good views of the buildings of Hinton Priory by following the right of way straight ahead before turning left towards the gatehouse.

Hinton Priory is the ruin of a former Carthusian priory founded in 1232 and abandoned at the dissolution of the monasteries some three centuries later. The remains are scanty compared to the great ruined abbeys of the North of England, though there are the remains of the chapter house, sacristy, refectory and a small portion of the church and cloisters are visible, as well as the outline of the cloisters, which measure 226 feet square. The nearby village of Hinton Charterhouse commemorates the Carthusian connection in its name, and the Priory owned much of the land in the area. The hamlet of Friary in the valley between Freshford and Iford (Walk 1), is so named because it once comprised living quarters for lay brothers from the Priory.

Cross the main road, turn right and sharp left by Abbey Lane, signposted to Sharpstone and Freshford. Once past the entrance to Homewood Park Hotel you can see Limpley Stoke church ahead. You begin to descend before the lane bears left; ignore the lane to the right (Rosemary Lane) and at the crossroads below go straight ahead (Ashe's Lane).

After a few yards you will find an indicated Public Footpath on the right. Cross the stone stile, follow the track until it bears right, and then keep to the footpath which continues straight ahead. There are three kissing gates and two more fields to cross before reaching Limpley Stoke church.

The Byway from Midford to Pipehouse.

11 NORTON ST. PHILIP

via Hinton Charterhouse

Distance:	4.5 miles
Maps:	Pathfinder 1199; Explorer 5
	Landranger 172
Map Reference:	774808
Refreshment en route:	The George and the Fleur de Lys at
	Norton St. Philip; The Rose and Crown
	at Hinton Charterhouse

THE WALK is a pleasant and varied one which could provide an enjoyable half day's ramble or even a whole day.

The route leaves Norton by a field path and thence by a quiet lane through a delightfully unspoilt valley, then through a wood where it follows a track up a hillside. Now the route traverses a plateau at around 400 feet, with wide views north and south, for almost a mile before reaching Hinton Charterhouse. From Hinton Church field paths are followed for over a mile, via Norwood Rare Breeds Farm, back to Norton St. Philip.

Norton St. Philip is best known for The George Inn, that magnificent hostelry at the centre of the village which must have been photographed and sketched a million times. The George is said to have been built by the monks of Hinton Charterhouse and there is certainly much of an ecclesiastical style about the detailing of the doors and windows of the stone-built ground floor. The inn was certainly used as a centre for the cloth trade; the top storey was once a great hall for the buying and selling of wool and cloth. The George has its associations with the famous too. Oliver Cromwell slept here when in pursuit of Charles II; the Duke of Monmouth stayed over on his ill-fated expedition – he was actually shot at through the

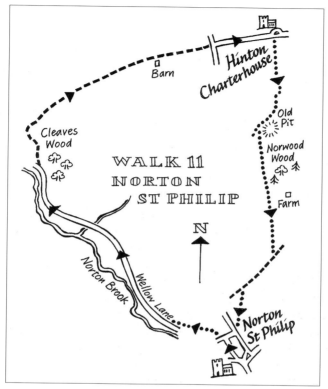

window of his room at the inn. Last but not least, Samuel Pepys ate and slept here and he records his satisfaction at doing so in his diary. The George Inn is a wonderful old building and it is well worth exploring the ground floor to which the pub user has access.

The view from the back of the George, where there is a garden, should also be savoured. The ground slopes down to a cricket pitch on Church Mead and beyond that is the church of St. Philip and St. James with its singular tower, said by some to have been constructed from fragments of the ruined priory at Hinton Charterhouse. There is a path on the right-hand side of the inn (as you face it) which leads down across Church Mead towards the church. Norton St. Philip is a sizeable village which retains its school (still in its original building of 1827) and Post Office. There are many attractive, stone-built houses and the pavements are made up of irregular stone flags.

To begin the walk: with your back to the entrance of the George Inn, bear left. Take the left fork downhill but, almost immediately, cross the road and turn right along North Street. At the end of North Street turn left by the lane leading downhill. Look out for a wooden stile beside a gate on the right at Lyde Green Cottage. Cross this stile and then another into the field; head straight across the field towards a gate (which may be obscured by vegetation in summer) in the far side.

Cross into the next field and follow the field boundary on the left, past the gate in the left-hand corner to reach a stile in the far corner just above the lane. Now head downhill towards a stile which drops you into the lane.

Turn right and continue along the lane for about a mile. Eventually you reach, on your left, a footbridge and ford across a stream. This provides a natural resting place but, once refreshed (I'm not suggesting you drink the stream-water!), continue by the lane until you arrive at a gate, stile and Public Footpath sign a little farther on. Enter the wood and keep to the main, well-marked, footpath which climbs the hillside.

A sign at the outset informs us that this wood is an S.S.S.I. – a Site of Special Scientific Interest, which basically means that nature is here happily left to her own devices. Early one May I found it alive with butterflies, especially brimstones and orange-tips, which seem to me to suit the English countryside much more than the more exotic tortoiseshells and peacocks. There are also some good growths of Star of Bethlehem, especially near the summit and at the beginning of the open track to Hinton Charterhouse. Another plant which I failed to recognise, but whose name I was given by someone accompanying me on the walk, is Chalkhill Milkwort. Whilst on the subject of wild flowers, you may have noticed the rather strange sight of Bath Asparagus growing in the hedgebanks beside the lane before reaching the footbridge. The flowers are supposed to taste like asparagus, though I remain unconvinced. Your pocket guide to wild flowers should certainly accompany you on this walk.

Footpath beside the George Inn, Norton St. Philip

Continue to follow the main track up the hillside until you leave the woods to enter a clearing; this is a peaceful spot indeed. Bear right here and leave the clearing by a stile beside a gate at the top right corner. Now follow this wide track leading between cornfields across a plateau towards Hinton Charterhouse. The Rose and Crown pub is opposite left.

At Hinton you cross the main road and continue by the lane opposite towards Hinton church.

Before you reach the church you should peer over the stone wall to catch sight of Hinton House, a most handsome edifice, set well back from the road and standing in its own extensive grounds. Pevsner tells us that the fine seven bay front dates from 1701.

The next stage of the route is indicated by a Public Footpath sign pointing across a stile on the right-hand side of the road, just before the turning which leads to Hinton Church. Enter the field here and make for the stile beside the oak tree ahead. Cross it to enter a fenced, linear plantation of mainly Christmas trees; follow the winding path until you reach the end and cross the stile.

Now head straight on across the field to reach a gate which leads into a wooded enclosure surrounding an overgrown sandpit. On reaching the sandpit you bear right to follow the hedgerow on the right.

You soon reach an open field. Here you turn left – as indicated by the yellow arrow on the fencepost at this point. You head across this large field towards a point on the far side just to the left of a pylon and just to the right of a wood.

Walk straight on beside the pylon to reach a stile in the field boundary; cross here and follow the field edge towards another stile, then a little to the right beside the wire fence to reach a stile, then across a ditch to another stile.

You are now in the environs of Norwood Rare Breeds Farm, which opens to the public and some of whose strange beasts you may observe in the fields hereabouts.

Bear right, with the windmill to your left, and cross four wooden step stiles in rapid succession until to reach the access road to the farm – here turn right.

Follow this lane for a short distance, keeping an eye open for a stile at the top of the bank on the left; this is found about twenty yards before the cottage. Cross into a field and turn right to cross the stile beside the cottage.

The right of way now follows the beaten path and heads diagonally across the field to reach a stile in the bottom left corner.

This reveals an interesting feature – an outcrop of rock which forms an extensive badger sett. Walking along here one May I found a badger carcass near the bottom of the field; I wondered whether he had been struck by a vehicle on the road and then tried to make his way home.

The stile at the bottom drops you onto the road which, bearing leftwards, takes you back into Norton St. Philip.

12 NUNNEY

via Lower Whatley, Egford, Vallis Vale,
Great Elm and Whatley

Distance:	Seven miles
Maps:	Pathfinder 1219; Explorer 5
	Landranger 183
Map Reference:	737457
Refreshment en route:	The Sun Inn at Whatley, on the last leg
	of the walk; the George at Nunney

THE WALK includes some pretty footpaths beside streams and some exhilarating stretches across fields. Unfortunately, there is no footpath between Lower Whatley and Egford and you are left with no alternative but to use the road for about a mile. However, this minor road provides a pleasant view over the valley of the Nunney Brook.

Nunney is a gem of a village, bypassed by the main road, its buildings charmingly grouped around the brook which flows towards the moat of Nunney Castle. The castle itself is surprising in being built where it is – not in some easily defendable, hill-top position but sitting low in a valley with a village about it. The castle is a ruin, but its four massive towers and curtain walls are pretty well intact, and the whole blends in remarkably well with the rest of the village and far from dominates the scene.

All Saints Church, opposite the castle, has a more commanding position than the castle; it is situated on a gentle slope overlooking the village. The church contains much of the thirteenth and fourteenth centuries; perhaps its most notable features are the monuments to be seen in the north aisle. They consist of a knight and lady of the fifteenth century and another couple of the Elizabethan period. There is also a fourteenth century knight lying

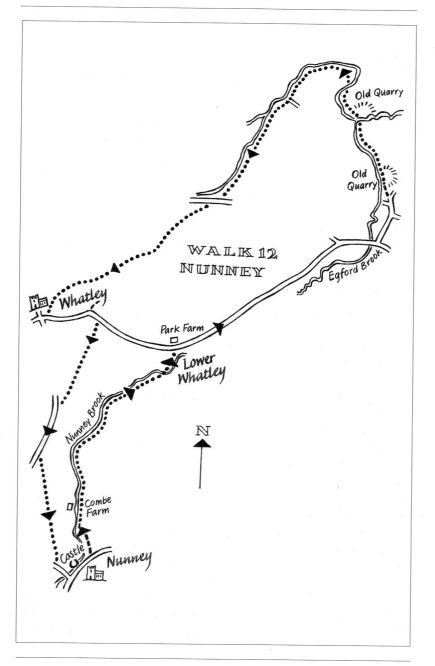

Old Quarry

Old Quarry

WALK 12 NUNNEY

Egford Brook

Whatley

Park Farm

Lower Whatley

Nunney Brook

N

Combe Farm

Castle

Nunney

on the windowsill behind. These stone sculptures provide an interesting study of evolving fashion in armour, dress and hairstyles.

- *From Nunney Castle and church, walk downstream beside Nunney Brook and take the first turning on the left towards Combe Farm. As you approach the farmhouse bear right over a stile and follow the beaten path as it heads downstream, with Nunney Brook on your left.*

  The water begins to flow much more slowly as you approach a weir by a footbridge. Cross the footbridge and turn right by the indicated right of way by the stile on the right. At the bridge ahead climb up to the drive and follow it to the left until you reach the lane. Turn right and follow the lane for about a mile past Egford Farm.

  Once across the stream you bear left; soon a lane joins from the right and your road swings uphill to the right. At this point head straight on along a centre track towards Vallis Farm. Cross the stile ahead and follow the footpath beside the stream.

You soon pass by a large, abandoned quarry on your right where you can see the tilted and folded strata of Carboniferous Limestone which in parts is stained yellow from the overlying Jurassic strata.

- *Continue to follow the footpath downstream until you cross a bridge by a confluence of streams.*

As you cross this bridge you will see, beyond the expanse of stone chippings, an outcrop of rock marking another former quarry. This site exhibits to perfection the horizontal Jurassic strata lying unconformably on the titled Carboniferous rocks.

- *From here you can either walk along the bed of the old railway track which left the main line just above Hapsford Bridge to run along Vallis Vale and Murder Combe to serve Whatley Quarry, or you can stick to the footpath beside the stream. If you follow the stream-side footpath you will notice that the direction of flow is now against you, rather than with you. This is no longer the Egford Brook, but*

*the water which flows from Murder Combe and Wadbury Valley
and which unite at Great Elm, a little upstream.*

Quarry showing unconformity in Vallis Vale

A little way along the footpath you will notice a number of old lime kilns which are still pretty well intact. The top of the kiln projects several feet over the base of the hopper where the burnt lime was extracted.

The footpath soon joins the former railway track and crosses the stream. You now follow the course of the old railway under a bridge beside the stream. Soon you pass under a new bridge which carries the railway, from a tunnel in the hill on your left, across the stream and into a tunnel through the hill on the opposite bank. This modern section of the railway line represents a rerouting of the branch line serving Whatley Quarry.

Follow the track of the old line beside the stream until you reach the road below Great Elm. Cross over and pass through the kissing gate opposite. Bear left by the right of way indicated as East Mendip

Way and Macmillan Way. Climb the slope to reach a level footpath; bear right.

This is an enjoyable stretch along the edge of the overgrown valley with views over the quarried slopes towards the wooded hill on which the Iron Age Tedbury Camp is sited.

The footpath emerges at a road between two enormous Mendip stone boulders. Here you bear left for a short distance before continuing along footpaths by turning right into the gap between hedges. These soon revert to a single field boundary which you follow on your left. At the next junction you cross the stile to the left and follow the hedge on your right.

You will see the spire of Whatley Church ahead and feel assured that you are heading straight towards it. Your progress may be interrupted by explosions from the huge quarry on the far side of the valley to your right. There is a wide view, especially to the south-east, where you can see the plateau on which Frome stands and, beyond Frome, you can see Cley Hill and the forested hills of Longleat.

Follow the hedgebank on the right until you reach the top right-hand corner of the field where you cross a stile into the adjoining field. Bear left towards the church.

The big house before the church is the old rectory and there is a ha ha between the house's garden and the cow field; that is, a sunken wall and ditch which ensures that the view from the garden is unimpaired but that beasts are confined to their field.

Traverse the field below the church to a stile in the paddock beside the church, then make for a stile into the churchyard itself.

Most of St. George's Church is the work of the Victorian restorers, although there are traces of the original thirteenth and fourteenth century work. The church is generally kept locked. Close by the church is Manor Farm which has seventeenth century mullioned windows. The gatehouse, with decorated arch, is older still.

Leave the church by the main gateway to the road and turn left. Follow the road towards the Sun Inn and leave the road by the lane which bears right, past the pub, towards the house beyond. Here cross the stile to the right of the house into the field; you now follow a field path for about half a mile.

Bear just a little to the left, heading down the slope until you locate an old iron kissing gate in the bottom right field corner. Once through here you head directly across the field to reach the road by a gate in the far right-hand corner, opposite Southfield House.

Bear left to follow the road for a few hundred yards until the next section of field path is reached, indicated on the left. Cross the stile to enter the field.

Once in this field you will see Nunney about half a mile ahead: the Castle with its massive round towers is most prominent. Walk diagonally across the field until the far boundary comes into view. Head straight across the next field, with Combe Farm to the left, towards a wooden stile. You now follow a well marked footpath into the village.

13 RODE

via Tellisford and River Frome

Distance:	3 miles
Maps:	Pathfinder 1199, 1200; Explorer 5
	Landranger 173, 183
Map Reference:	805540
Refreshment en route:	The Mill at Rode

THE WALK is a short one which completes a loop north of Rode by paths beside the River Frome, then across an old packhorse bridge and up through the hamlet of Tellisford, then back by field paths to Rode Mill, recently restored and converted into a large pub.

This short walk is most enjoyable. The quiet stretch from Langham House to Langham Farm is followed by the roar and excitement of the wier and a delightful riverside stretch. The traffic-free Tellisford Bridge and the climb uphill past old houses may be followed by a detour to visit Tellisford Church. There follows a series of field paths, sufficiently elevated to afford sweeping views down towards the River Frome flowing in the valley bottom. Finally, there is the prospect of the former cloth mill at Rode, now a pub complete with revolvong waterwheel, then the old bridge across the Frome, just wide enough to accept traffic in single-file.

The A361, though it passes close to St. Laurence Church, bypasses the village, as does the B3109 to Bradford on Avon. There is usually space to park your car in the vicinity of the small, triangular village green, with a war memorial at its centre.

The prospect of rows of old stone houses from here is an enticing one and you may like to start the walk with a short perambulation of Rode itself. To do so, head towards the village centre. Notice the

---

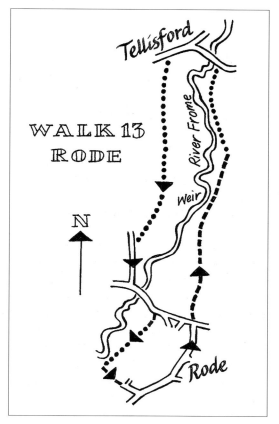

WALK 13
RODE

N

Tellisford

River Frome

Weir

Rode

old Baptist Chapel, dated 1780, and adjacent school room, dated 1839. Farther on, past the pub, in the vicinity of some industrial buildings and set back from the street on the left, is an old Methodist Chapel, dated 1809. You can return to the village green by the lower street through the village by taking the left fork at the pub.

You might explore further by walking out of the village centre towards the old parish church on the A361. St. Laurence dates from the fourteenth century though it was heavily restored by the Victorians. The clerestory windows and arcading render it a light and airy building. There is an interesting painting on display of the village men holding hands and dancing in a circle round the church. This ancient custom apparently had pagan origins, like so much of what is considered to be 'Christian tradition'. Known as 'clipping the church', it was enacted on Shrove Tuesday night for the avowed purpose of driving out the devil, and survived in many parts of Wessex until the nineteenth century.

* *From the village green, head northwards out of the village but uphill,*
* *towards the main road. Cross the road and follow the track left beside*
* *the entrance drive to Langham House, signposted Langham Place.*

Langham House was formerly Rode Hill House, the scene of a notorious murder in Victorian times. This story has been recounted often, most recently as 'The Unsolved Mystery of Rode' in a collection entitled *West Country Treasury* (Ex Libris Press, 1989).

You will also certainly notice the twin towers of Christ Church, Rode's other church, built in 1824 and described by Pevsner as 'amazing', up the hill on your right.

* *Follow the metalled track as it follows the River Frome downstream*
* *towards Tellisford. Eventually the track forks – take the left fork*
* *towards Langham Farm. Follow the right of way to the right and*
* *enter the field beyond by the gate. Now simply follow the river*
* *downstream, by a riverside meadow, a stile, past a pill box and weir,*
* *until you reach the pack horse bridge at Tellisford.*
*   *Climb the stile and turn left to cross the bridge. On the far side*
* *you can hear the rush of water as it tumbles through the ivy-clad*
* *ruins of old Tellisford Mill.*

First mention of Tellisford Mill was in 1574, when it was held by a Trowbridge clothing family from the Hungerfords of Farleigh Castle.

* *Continue the walk by climbing the slope by the flight of old stone*
* *steps past the mill. There are some attractive houses to be seen here.*

Opposite Glebe Farm there is the beginning of a right of way through fields to Rock Farm, on the lane near Rode Bridge. You may first care to take an optional detour to visit Tellisford Church. To do so, simply continue walking uphill: the church is set back to the right of

Tellisford Bridge, looking across the River Frome from Somerset to Wiltshire.

the crossroads at the summit. However, it is more interesting to approach the church by field path. In this case, once past Top Farm, on your right, look out for a stile. Cross here to follow the right of way to the churchyard wall, where a massive stone stile greets you.

Tellisford Church was much restored by the Victorians, but it must not be dismissed as unworthy of a visit (indeed, a church is always much more than a building!) All Saints is diminutive, consisting only of tower, nave and chancel and possesses a simplicity which is immediately appealing. There is a Norman arch with zigzag pattern over the door and some interesting fragments of sculpture inside which originated from the old village cross which was situated near the church from the fourteenth century. These fragments were discovered in the fabric of the church during nineteenth-century restoration work.

Now to continue the main route from Glebe Farm House: When you enter the field you will soon notice the beaten path diverging, with one way heading down towards the river, the other heading straight on. Better to head in a line across the centre of the field towards an old stone slab standing, quite isolated, near the field's centre.

This must have been a stone slab stile in a hedgerow hereabouts – indeed, if you look to right and left you will see several overgrown stumps marking the sites of trees which stood in the hedgerow here; a nice example of footpath archaeology.

From here carry on in the same direction towards the hedgerow. Now you must descend the hillside to reach a gap in the barbed wire fence which allows the right of way to cross the ditch and reach a stile on the opposite side. Follow the direction of the indicated Public Footpath sign to ascend the slope, then bear left with a hedgerow to your left and the bosky slope to your left.

Pass through a gap in the hedge and head straight on towards another stile, then another and another. At the third stile you must change course: turn right up a fenced track. At a point where the track bends to the right look out for a stile on the left. Cross here and bear left past a bungalow, then descend to reach a stile which drops you onto the lane. Turn left to reach the road by The Mill.

Now restored and converted into a very large pub, this former woollen mill stood empty and abandoned for many years until its recent resurrection. It is well worth exploring – sup a refreshing drink while you gaze in awe at the massive waterwheel in the basement and watch the waters of the River Frome flow beneath the undershot wheel. Records of a mill here date back to the sixteenth century, though most of the present building was a factory built at the beginning of the nineteenth century.

Cross the bridge, past a handsome Georgian house and a group of buildings which includes stables and a summer house with a Venetian window.

Bear right along the footpath a short distance up from the river and follow this fenced right of way as it follows an even contour just above the River Frome. It eventually meets a T-junction where you turn left, uphill, towards the outskirts of Rode. Turn left to reach the main street through the village.

14 SOUTH WRAXALL

*via Monkton Farleigh, Farleigh Wick,
and Great Cumberwell*

Distance:	7.5 miles
Maps:	Pathfinder 1184
	Landranger 173
Map Reference:	833648
Refreshment en route:	The Long Arms at South Wraxall;
	The King's Arms at Monkton Farliegh;
	The Fox and Hounds at Farleigh Wick;
	This could turn into a pub crawl!

THE WALK, though a good distance, does not entail any steep slopes. Most of the route is by field paths and green tracks, with a shorter section along lanes which carry little traffic. South Wraxall and Monkton Farleigh are both attractive and interesting villages.

> *To begin the walk, make for the centre of South Wraxall, in the vicinity of the pub and church.*

South Wraxall is a scattered village: the distance between the Manor House and the farm to the north and Home Farm to the south is about a mile on foot and rather further by road. There are, in fact, three distinct nuclei to the village: the Manor House and Farm form a northerly group, the church and pub a central group, whilst Lower Wraxall comprises a number of farms, houses and cottages.

St. James Church is most notable for its tower with prominent stair turret and saddle-back roof. The tower dates from c. 1300; Pevsner describes it as 'picturesque', but I find that the introduction of oblique angles into a structure whose lines are essentially vertical lends a jarring note. Sorry! Inside, the church houses the Long Chapel, where

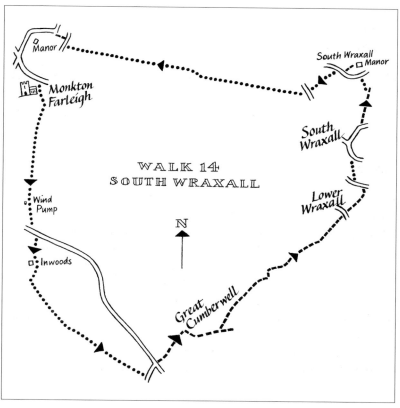

generations of lords of the Manor of South Wraxall lie interred.

Take the lane opposite the Long Arms pub beside the church. The lane eventually bears right: just after this bend look out for a turning on the left, beside Willow Cottage, and follow the track round towards the furthest cottage ahead. Follow the right of way just to the left of these three cottages and then cross the two stiles and follow the field boundary on the left to a stile in the top left corner — here you enter the lane outside South Wraxall Manor House.

Pevsner says of South Wraxall Manor that 'the house is an outstandingly successful mixture of the fifteenth century and the later Elizabethan and Jacobean. Moreover, what features of both periods remain are outstanding in their own right.' However, the house is privately owned and is not open to the public. The little that can be seen is certainly enticing: the gate house with immaculate oriel window over the archway, the enormous drawing-room window on the west front, which was added to the north of the hall in the late sixteenth century and, in the garden facing the road, the domed, octagonal summer house. South Wraxall Manor was the home of the Longs from the early fifteenth century until quite recently in the present century. It is said that the first tobacco smoked in England was smoked here.

Beyond the Manor to the east is the Manor Farm, the farmhouse of which was originally a hospice for poor travellers and dates from the fourteenth century. Little or nothing of this is visible from the road, however.

Bear left along the lane for a short distance. Just past the farmhouse enter the field on the left by the gate. Go straight across the field to the rough wooden stile in the opposite boundary. Enter the next field beside the old shed on your left, behind which you cross a couple of stiles. Carry on until you reach the lane by a gate.

The pair of iron gates and gateposts opposite originally formed part of the grand drive between Monkton Farleigh and South Wraxall Manors. Cross the wooden stile just beyond the far gatepost and proceed to walk the one and a third miles straight ahead to the lane below Monkton Farleigh Manor, whose Georgian façade is clearly visible on elevated ground in the distance. You cross a couple of stiles on the way to reach a stile beside a cottage below the big house.

The most direct route from here to the church and the village main street is to turn left and then right. However, there are objects of interest to be seen by making a circular tour of the village. To do so, bear right on reaching the lane below the Manor House, then left up the lane signposted to Manor Farm until you reach a lane joining from the right.

Opposite this is a Public Footpath sign indicating a right of way to Kingsdown. Go through the attractive kissing gate here into the field where you may observe the recently tidied up and fenced off remains of ancient fish ponds.

St. James Church, South Wraxall

These were installed by the monks of the Cluniac priory of Monkton Farleigh, founded in 1125, and sited where the Manor House now stands. Little evidence remains of the priory, save for a few stone fragments, a pair of lancet windows and some thirteenth-century stone effigies. None of this is visible from the road.

Walk around the pond and leave the field by the kissing gate beyond to reach the lane once more, where it bears left to follow the boundary wall of the Manor.

Once past the cottages on the right, you can see, at the far side of the field to your right, a small, solitary building with a steep pitched roof. This is the ancient Monks Conduit, where a spring of water was utilised to supply the priory and still does supply the Manor.

Bear left at the road ahead, opposite the Kings Arms pub.

This is the village main street, with the stone cottages falling away to St. Peter's Church which, apart from its thirteenth-century tower, was largely rebuilt by the Victorians. One unusual feature is the holy-water stoop set into the wall at the entrance gate.

Immediately beyond the church, take the signposted Public Footpath to Farleigh Wick. Beyond the churchyard you cross a stile into a field, then follow the barbed-wire fence on the right towards a kissing gate in the hedgerow. Cross the track and leg it over the rather high wooden bar opposite into the next field and make for a stile near the bottom corner, then follow the hedgebank on the left. At the top left corner cross into a further field and follow the hedgebank on your left.

Bear left to follow the field boundary until you reach an improvised Footpath sign indicating that the right of way follows the hedgerow on your right. You will see the wind pump straight ahead, also the twin gables of a white painted house to the left of the Fox and Hounds at Farleigh Wick. Go through a gap in the hedge, then across the open field towards the delapidated field boundary opposite, then through a further gap and on beside the wind pump. The exit is by a stile set in the far left corner beside the main road.

To continue the walk, cross the road and bear left towards the gateway with stone pillars. Enter the gateway, where the right of way is indicated, and walk up the drive towards 'Inwoods'. Where the drive forks, bear left towards the group of buildings ahead. Pass through the gate on the left and into a field. Turn right and follow the boundary wall of Inwoods. Bear left at the top right hand corner of this field towards the gate below. Once through the gate you keep to the left and head down towards a solidly built wooden stile.

The next section of the walk is not so easy to navigate, so please PAY ATTENTION. You need to continue in the same south-westerly direction: as you head across the field by the beaten track the far boundary will soon hove into view. When you are about half-way between it and the stile you have just crossed, stop in your tracks. Look to the left and you will see a row of young trees in the boundary. Change direction and head towards these. You will find the crossing point into the next field roughly in the middle of this outcrop of trees. Now start climbing directly up the slope. Once the far boundary comes into view head for the gap, just to the right of the largest tree. As you approach you will spot the Footpath notice. Drop onto the lane here and bear left to reach the main road once again.

Cross the road and take the track opposite towards Great Cumberwell Farm (to the left of the grandiose entrance to Cumberwell Park Golf Club). Head towards the Golf Club's great 'barn' but, before reaching it, turn right along the high stone wall. This leads you past Great Cumberwell Farm with its enormous heap of discarded agricultural machinery and, opposite the Weighbridge and wasteland of the Landfill site. Head left where the track forks and carry straight on towards Cherry Orchard Farm, where the track leads directly to South Wraxall.

At Lower Wraxall cross the lane and carry straight on by another lane, then through a kissing gate into a field. Follow the path to another gate and bear left by the sixteenth-century Mison's Farm. Cross the road to another well-marked path and through three kissing gates to Church Fields and the pub and church at the centre of the village.

15 SOUTHSTOKE

via Tucking Mill, Midford and the Somerset Coal Canal

Distance:	4.5 miles
Maps:	Pathfinder 1183; Explorer 155
	Landranger 172
Map Reference:	747613
Refreshment en route:	The Packhorse in Southstoke
	Hope and Anchor at Midford,
	about half-way

The walk is full of interest and variety, as well as much beautiful and unspoilt countryside, though we are never very far from the southern fringes of Bath. The going is fairly easy though there is a sharp ascent back to Southstoke at the end of the walk.

Southstoke is an attractive village set in a hollow between Odd Down and Hodshill, its buildings well grouped around the crossroads and small sloping green at its centre. St. James Church has a low perpendicular tower; its main feature of interest is its intricately carved Norman doorway. The carvings have rather too crisp edges, probably indicating work done during the restoration of 1845 – indeed, the entire right hand pillar was replaced at that time. Sketches on display inside show the church after the 1712 rebuilding and before and after the 1845 restoration. Beyond the church is Manor Farm and barn. The barn dates from c. 1500 and includes a dovecote, still used as such, beyond the central porch.

To begin the walk, leave the village by the lane at the top of the green which leads away from the village in the opposite direction to the church, i.e. in an easterly direction. After about a quarter of a mile look for a gap in the hedge on the left where a signposted public

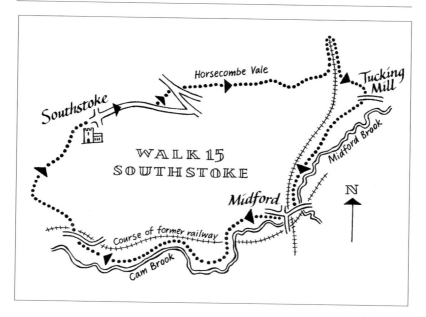

footpath leads through a kissing gate and across a field to a gate in the far right hand corner.

Cross Old Midford Road, then the main road and make for the signpost and stile on the opposite side. Cross the stile and follow the hedgerow on the left. Now simply follow the beaten path downhill through a succession of fields, bearing a little to the right at a stile, until you reach the valley bottom, and the footbridge (a couple of railway sleepers) across the stream. Bear right to enter a wood by a stile.

Notice the boundary stone on your left, dated 1894, and marking the boundary between the City of Bath and Somerset.

Follow the path along the valley, slightly above the stream, first through a wood, then across a field, then again through woods. You emerge from this last section of wood to find a group of buildings before you. These form part of the Wessex Water Authority's complex at Tucking Mill. Cross a stream flowing from the left, then turn left up the valley. You pass through an iron squeezer stile – here notice the old railway track-bed to the right.

This marks the course of the old Somerset and Dorset branch railway – at first an embankment and then a cutting as the line prepared to enter the tunnel under Combe Down. The squeezer stile is just about at the point where the transition from embankment to cutting occurs.

Turn right and right again at a pair of kissing gates just above the tunnel entrance. Now descend by a footpath on the east side of the cutting. Keep to the right, beside the wooded slope. The footpath enters woods by a stile and diverges to the left above Tucking Mill reservoir. Continue to descend – past a house and then on to a lane.

Here you cross to the far side, turn right and almost immediately locate the right of way just to the left of the hedge.

Notice the house across the lane on your right – its front wall bears a tablet commemorating the fact that William Smith lived here when he was employed as engineer on the Somerset Coal Canal. William Smith is known as the 'Father of English Geology' because he it was who established the orderly succession of strata in the earth's crust and that each layer may be identified by the fossil remains it contains. Smith went on to conduct a geological survey of the country around Bath and drew some of the first geological maps. These may be seen in the geological collection at Bath Reference Library.

Another signpost at the entrance to Tuckingmill Reservoir bears the message 'Disabled Fishing' which does not mean, as someone has suggested, that anglers must employ straight hooks.

Now simply follow the beaten path through the undergrowth until you eventually emerge at the main road at Midford.

This footpath follows the course of the old Somerset Coal Canal. This is not immediately obvious but after a few hundred yards the recognisable cross-section of a canal situated in a river valley becomes clear. To your left is a man-made embankment which drops away to the riverside meadow. To your right is the shallow basin of the canal, whilst you are walking along the old towpath. The Midford Brook from Midford itself down to the Avon marks the former boundary of

Bridge over disused Somerset Coal Canal, near Midford

Somerset and Wiltshire, so that Limpley Stoke and the hill behind are in Wiltshire.

> *On reaching the main road at Midford turn right. The next stage of the route is indicated by a signpost opposite the Hope and Anchor pub.*

The two disused railway viaducts at Midford are like a couple of stranded dinosaurs of the railway age. The larger one beside the pub carried the Somerset and Dorset line from Bath, whilst the smaller, which no longer spans the road, carried the Cam Valley line from Limpley Stoke.

> *Follow the footpath under the viaduct. Cross the wooden stile and soon emerge into the open; once again you are following the towpath of the canal.*

Along the first few yards of the towpath you may notice the exposed rockface on the opposite bank. These strata are the Midford Sands, a friable sandstone which is a local variation in the Liassic formation. The bridge over the Cam Brook on the left marks the course of an aborted branch of the Somerset Coal Canal: this once grandiose river crossing was as far as it got. Farther along, just before the railway embankment, which is built across the canal and completely blocks it off, there is another stone bridge looking very forlorn as it spans a dried-out and grassed-over canal bed in a cow field (illustration page 99).

You must now cross the railway by passing under the bridge section over the Cam Brook. Cross the stile ahead and bear left towards the stream, then right along the water's edge and under the railway bridge. Bear right past the bridge, then left over a wooden stile to continue the walk along the towpath.

This section through unspoilt country is the most rewarding of the walk. Following wet weather the canal is full of water and really looks like a canal.

Further along you encounter a series of three locks, the stonework now fairly delapidated and overgrown. After the third lock the towpath reaches a wooden stile. Cross the stile and turn right. Immediately look out for a stile on the left; cross here and follow the right of way towards the buildings ahead. Cross one stile and bear right to reach the lane by a stile. Head under the brick railway arch.

Here is an interesting plaque which relates the history of the Somerset Coal Canal, in particular the various attempts which were made to overcome the problem of raising barges at this point.

Follow the canal towpath once again, keeping the basin and locks to your left. After five such locks, the canal takes a hairpin bend to the left through the woods.
To return to Southstoke cross the stile ahead and follow the path

keeping the stream on your left. The path bears right to ascend the hill, passing to the left of a house, then along a track by the edge of a wood. Climb the field ahead and make for an iron squeezer stile at the top. This drops you into a lane which leads directly to Southstoke – the barn, the church and the green in the village centre (and the Packhorse pub hidden away along the lane to the right below the village green).

GREEN LANE

16 St. CATHERINE'S

via St. Catherine's Valley

Distance:	3 miles
Maps:	Pathfinder 1167; Explorer 155
	Landranger 172
Map Reference:	777703
Refreshment en route:	Alas, none.

THE WALK begins in the valley at St. Catherine's Court and soon climbs a lane to reach the plateau. There follow hedged tracks, field paths, wooded sections and inspiring views. The whole area, no more than two miles from the centre of Bath, is deeply rural and could be a hundred miles from a place of any size.

The walk begins at St. Catherine's Court, where the group of buildings includes the big house, the tithe barn and the church (which alone is open to the public). Parking on the lane in St. Catherine's Valley can be a problem. The lane widens near the Court and it is advisable to park under the trees before the Court gates are reached.

St. Catherine's was originally a possession of Bath Abbey, the Court and church being built in the late 1400's. According to a leaflet written and kindly supplied by the present owner, the building dates from the fifteenth century, with the exception of the library wing and the orangery, which were added in 1919 but built in the original Tudor style.

St. Catherine's Church contains a representation of Prior Cantlow in the fine stained glass dated 1490. There is an impressive monument to William Blanchard (died 1631), and his wife, in the form of two life-size kneeling figures on the north side of the chancel. The whole

group at St. Catherine's – the Court, the church and the tithe barn forms a most beautiful ensemble, the weathered stone of these attractive old buildings set against the green, wooded hillside. The best view is perhaps from the footpath below, approaching from the south, a point included in the route of this walk.

To begin the walk, make for the kissing gate just beyond the entrance to St. Catherine's Court. Go through here to enter the field which reaches down to St. Catherine's Brook. Head diagonally – half-left, in line with the telegraph pole – across the field, by the beaten path, until you reach a stile in the hedgerow as it descends to the brook.

Cross this stile and head down towards the footbridge at the bottom of the garden. Cross the stile to enter the riverside meadow. Bear left and follow the beaten path downstream, above the trees.

St. Catherine's Church seen through the gateposts to the Court

- *You reach a stile and cross a tributary stream flowing from the right,*
- *then over another couple of stiles to follow the tributary upstream.*
- *Follow the enclosed footpath until you reach the lane, where you*
- *turn right, past Ayford Farm. The lane now climbs, quite steeply.*

This is the best kind of country lane – deep sunken; vegetation trying to force its way through along the centre; much growth on banks that the hedge-cutter does not seem to reach until the summer's end – and scarcely a hint of traffic.

Carry on until the lane begins to flatten out and keep your eyes skinned for a bridleway on your right. When you spot it you turn sharp right and follow this double-hedged track above a steep slope at the head of the valley. The track eventually becomes more open but continues in the same direction along a field boundary.

You emerge onto the lane at Ashwicke Home Farm. Turn right at the lane and follow it past the farm buildings until you reach an indicated Public Footpath leading into the field on your right. Climb over the stile and bear left to follow the beaten path through the field towards the woods below – in the far bottom corner.

You soon emerge into the open on a bulbous promontory which is a perfect place to sit and stare – you begin to feel that here you are truly in the foothills of the Cotswolds.

Climb directly down the hillside, following the same general direction. The path becomes beaten where it heads for a gap in the wood. Cross the stile, then turn left on reaching the driveway.

Turn right at the lane. After a short distance, look out for a steel gate, marked as a right of way, on the right. Squeeze through a gap to the left of the gate and cross the stile which is found a little way on the left.

Now follow the beaten path towards a gate; cross here, and follow the edge of the field to a gap in the hedge and stile beyond. Bear right just before the partially built structure ahead. Note the plaque set into the gable on the far side – one wonders whether this half-finished house will remain so.

Head to the right of the outhouse, then follow the beaten path across the next field to reach a gate in the hedgerow on the far side. From here you can see St. Catherine's Court on the far side of the valley.

Follow the valley, crossing two more stiles, until you reach the footbridge at the bottom of the garden which you crossed at the beginning of the walk. Simply retrace your steps back to the lane.

17 STEEPLE ASHTON

via East Town and Stourton Water

Distance:	4 miles
Maps:	Pathfinder 1200
	Landranger 173
Map Reference:	905571
Refreshment en route:	The Long Arms in Steeple Ashton

THE WALK is an easy half day's ramble with no steep climbs. It passes through open, arable fields and gives some fine views towards Salisbury Plain. Interest is added at the half-way stage at Stourton Water, a large pond fed by a tributary of the Biss Brook and a haven for wildlife.

Steeple Ashton is one of Wiltshire's most attractive villages and one of its best conserved, as the plaques opposite the village green which record several successes in the Best Kept Village competition testify.

The church is stunning: its numerous pinnacles leap up like so many exclamation marks and compel the passer-by to gaze long and admiringly. St. Mary's is a large and magnificent church and a reminder of the great prosperity which the wool and cloth trade brought to this community in the past. Inside the church there is stone vaulting in all parts but the nave, which has a wooden roof. The steeple, which formerly reached a height of 186 feet, collapsed in 1670.

In addition to the church, this sizeable village exhibits a collection of houses notable in their variety of periods, styles and building materials. There are houses built of stone, but also of brick; there are some of both materials. There are one or two stone roofs, but more of tile or slate or thatch. There are cruck-built cottages, timber-framed houses and scaled-down Georgian town houses. There is a village green with a blind house and a village cross, dated 1679, with a sundial.

There is usually space to park in the lane leading down to the church. If you are starting from the church, you should head back to the main street, turn left and carry on past the village green and the pub. Ignore the public footpath sign indicating a right of way to the right, just past the pub, but walk on a few yards and turn right into Acreshort Lane.

Proceed along here until the bungalows give way to fields and views onwards towards the escarpment of Salisbury Plain and the villages along its foot. After half a mile or so you reach a junction of ways where you turn right by the track signposted as a bridleway leading to East Town Farm. Follow this track through the fields, first down, then through a dog-leg bend right and left, and up again towards East Town Farm, easily identified by its wind pump.

Walk through the farm buildings and past the cottages to reach the lane where you bear right. You can see, to your left, across the grounds of Rood Ashton Park and, closer to hand, the collapsed brick wall of an enclosed garden beside Home Farm.

Follow the lane down to a dip where willows and reeds grow and the lane crosses a brook by a bridge. The wooded area to the left is Stourton Water, the presence of water hinted at by the fishing notices hereabouts. Here is a junction of ways – to the right is Sandpits Lane leading back to Steeple Ashton; straight on is Mudmead Lane, the next stage of the route; to the left is an indicated right of way to Trowbridge.

Before heading on by Mudmead Lane, it is definitely worth crossing the stile into the field on your left in the direction of Trowbridge. A few yards along you will be rewarded with a glimpse of Stourton Water. This is a beautiful stretch of water and is a good place to stand still and wait for the wildlife – you are almost bound to see the fish jumping and a kingfisher or two flash silently above the water. The muddy banks of this little lake are also a good place to look for those plants which prefer such a habitat.

Continue in the same direction by the hedged but unmetalled track which climbs out of this dip, straight ahead.

This is the sort of old byway where one expects to come across an encampment of gypsies. Indeed, the extension of this lane on the far side of Steeple Ashton is named on the Pathfinder map as 'Gipsies' Lane (Track)'. Mudmead Lane today is sadly neglected. The way resembles an obstacle course in places, though it is never impassable, as a result of collapsed trees from the hedgerows either side. The wild flowers prosper here, with one species dominating for a stretch, then another – there is a vigorous growth of comfrey in the lower reaches – as do the butterflies when conditions are right. These old, sunken, and half-forgotten ways act as a kind of linear nature reserve nestling among the vast, prairie-like fields which surround them.

The village green, Steeple Ashton

You quite suddenly emerge from the undergrowth to witness a wide view south-eastwards across the fields towards the village and the escarpment beyond. Carry on – the track levels out and eventually reaches a section which is evidently used by wheeled vehicles.

Look out for the public footpath signs along here and turn right into the field towards the village. Follow the track between crops and continue in the same direction towards a low brick building – marked on the Pathfinder map as Reservoir. Make for a stile just beyond the left hand side of this building. Cross here and follow the field boundary on your left. You reach a stile beside a gate on your left – cross here to enter built-up Steeple Ashton. Turn left at the T-junction ahead and you very soon reach the main road.

You can reach the village centre by simply turning right, but there is a pleasanter way back to the church by crossing the road and climbing the stile opposite. From here you cross the field towards the church and head for the road by the passage which is found beside the church wall on the right.

18 UPTON SCUDAMORE

via Norrdge, Chapmanslade and Thoulstone

Distance:	6 miles
Map:	Pathfinder 1200
	Landranger 183
Map Reference:	865477
Refreshment en route:	Three Horseshoes in Upton Scudamore;
	The Angel Inn in Chapmanslade

THE WALK is a relatively long one along old tracks and field paths, with a little road walking. There is a real sense of remoteness from the workaday world along much of this route. The field paths and tracks from Norridge Farm to the lane below Chapmanslade are a delight and the thickly enclosed track which stretches from Thoulstone Farm to the lane near Upton Scudamore, with occasional glimpses over wide, empty corn fields, has a real touch of mystery about it.

Upton Scudamore is so named because it is situated some four hundred feet up on a spur of lower chalk which juts out to the west from Salisbury Plain; the Scudamores were lords of the manor since Norman times. The village church of St. Mary was largely rebuilt by the Victorians, and the plain tower a century before, although it does retain a good Norman arch. There are few buildings of antiquity in this rather workaday village though the Manor Farmhouse is partly medieval.

Outside the church the road is wide enough to allow parking. With your back to Upton Scudamore church, turn left along the lane and carry on until the road swings away to the right. Make for the stile and signpost at this point. It is worth pausing here to take in the

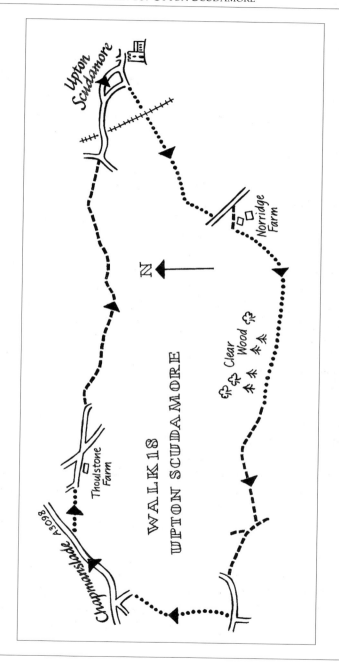

wide view and plot your course ahead. The wooded eminence of Arn Hill is to your left, the Warminster by-pass below, the wooded grounds of Longleat, the isolated knoll of Cley Hill, Norridge Wood and Clear Wood ahead on the far side of the A36.

Your way is straight ahead, first across the old bridge over the railway. Immediately you will notice a yellow arrow indicating the right of way to the left of the fence; at the end of this field cross the stile and carry on in the same direction. Cross the next stile ahead and follow the field boundary on your right. At the end of this field there is neither stile nor obvious crossing point to reach the last field before reaching the main road. It is therefore necessary to scramble across the ditch and up the bank to cross the barbed wire fence where there is a gap in the hedge. Now head diagonally across this last field towards the far left corner near an old tree stump. Cross the fence to reach a redundant bit of the A36. Turn left and climb the double step stile to reach the road, cross over (with care!) and head along the grass verge to reach Norridge Farm.

Turn right into the farm and follow the concrete track past the farm buildings, to a point where it bears left, just before a white painted wall and entrance to a driveway, through a couple of gates to enter a field. Follow the wheel tracks diagonally across this field to reach the far right corner. Take the gate on the right leading into a long narrow field. Follow the field boundary on your right until you leave the field to follow a wide track with Clear Wood on your right and a hedgerow on your left.

The track eventually emerges into a field; follow the right of way along the right hand boundary. When the field ends, follow the beaten path into the trees on your right, then through a broken gate to leave the wood behind you.

Now you can see Chapmanslade straight ahead – a long line of buildings standing prominently on the ridge about a mile to the north-west. The western tip of Chapmanslade is in Somerset; Frome is about three miles further west.

Simply follow the hedgerow on your left, descending slightly, until you reach a hedged track below. Bear right at the cross track. A little further there is a junction of tracks and the entrances to three fields. Take the left fork and follow this until you reach the lane beside a barn. Turn left here.

Follow the lane until you can see a post box on the triangle ahead. Just before this look out for the footpath sign indicating a narrow path uphill on your right. Climb the stile at the top and cross the field to reach the stile in the fence further on. Walk straight on towards two spreading willow trees where you will find a stile just to their left. Now follow the beaten path to reach the track where you turn left past houses to reach a triangle at the road through Chapmanslade.

Chapmanslade is built on a ridge formed by an outcrop of Upper Greensand. The place name Chapmanslade literally means 'the road of the chapmen', or pedlars, and one can imagine the long road crossing the county boundary and linking Westbury and Frome being a favourite meeting place for traders.

Old granary, Thoulstone Farm, near Chapmanslade

Turn left if you want the pub but right to continue the walk. There is a pavement on the left: carry on past Dead Maids Farm and turn left along the lane towards Thoulstone Farm.

The house at the junction to the left is known by the unusual name of Dead Maids. The origin of this name lies in a rather gruesome story which begins in Black Dog Wood, a little to the north. A local farmer's daughter had two suitors, each unknown to the other, one of whom owned a black dog. When they discovered each other's intentions the two men fought until the owner of the dog was killed. At this the dog killed his master's slayer and the farmer's daughter committed suicide and was buried at Dead Maids Cross (according to Kathleen Wiltshire in her book, *Ghosts and Legends of the Wiltshire Countryside*, 1973).

An interesting feature at Thoulstone is to be seen on the left of the drive just beyond the farmhouse. There is an old granary still intact: a wooden structure standing upon staddle stones. Staddle stones are, of course, a favourite piece of garden furniture and one can find them in many pub and private gardens in the countryside. But here they are still in their original position: supporting a wooden granary and protecting grain, once stored here, from vermin.

Cross the A36 (again, with care) and take the first turning on the left, which is indicated as a cul de sac. Just past Thoulstone Park Farm the metalled road bends to the right, but you bear to the left along a stony track which is signposted as a bridleway. Quite soon the chippings abate and the track becomes a lovely green tunnel leading directly back between fields towards Upton Scudamore.

You eventually emerge at a junction of lanes. Cross over and take the lane opposite which leads across the railway line directly to Upton Scudamore and the village church.

Looking out from Stoney Littleton long barrow (Walk 19)

19 WELLOW

via Baggridge Hill and Stoney Littleton

Distance:	6 miles
Maps:	Pathfinder 1199
	Landranger 172
Map Reference:	741583
Refreshment en route:	The Fox and Badger at Wellow

THE WALK is a pleasing and varied one, and has a surprisingly remote feel. The route leaves Wellow to follow the Wellow Brook downstream, then heads up a tributary valley towards Norton St. Philip, branching off to climb Baggridge Hill and reach a point above five hundred feet. From here the descent is through a wood, then by a bridleway and fieldpath, via Stoney Littleton Long Barrow, and back to Wellow. It is advisable to take a torch on this ramble if you wish to explore the inner recesses of Stoney Littleton Long Barrow, and it is quite safe to do so.

Wellow is a spacious and attractive village and an essentially linear one which stretches for over half a mile along a road which is parallelled by the course of the former Cam Valley branch railway. The village is situated on a south-facing slope at between two and three hundred feet, and there are a few more cottages beside the lane which leads down to the ford and footbridge across Wellow Brook.

The pride of Wellow is its very handsome church, which stands in a commanding position at the northern edge of the village. The church dates back to 1372, which is a comparatively late date for the origin of the village churches visited on these rambles. Wellow, in fact, is one of the very few villages in the area which is not mentioned in the Domesday Book.

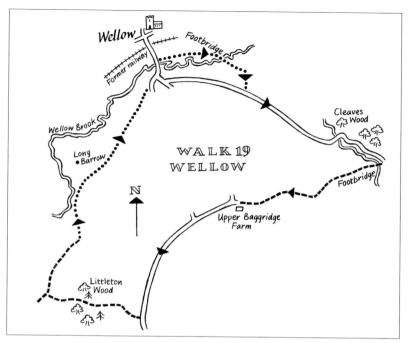

St. Julian's Church is particularly attractive inside because of the architectural consistency it displays – this in place of the jumble of periods and styles to which one is accustomed in village churches. The chancel was, in fact, rebuilt in 1890 but is a sympathetic restoration. The clerestory windows throw ample light on the uncluttered interior. The intricate carving of the rood screen and the colourful sculptures in the Hungerford chapel provide a striking contrast to the bare grey stone of the main structure. This really is an outstanding church which you should take time to enjoy.

To begin the walk, take the lane leading down beside the village school past the twin piers of the former railway bridge, and down towards Wellow Brook.

Just before the ford, look out for a stile on the left: cross over here to enter a field. Wellow Brook meanders its way down the valley to the right – simply follow the general eastward course of the brook without sticking to its every twist and turn.

Carry on across a second field, then into a third. Look out for a footbridge across the stream.

Once on the opposite bank, the right of way crosses and climbs the field diagonally to the left to reach the row of trees on the hillside. Follow the trees to the left to reach a stile to enter a field on your right; then follow the hedgebank on your right uphill to reach the lane opposite Wellow Farm. Turn left and follow the lane for about a mile, past Norton Lane Farm, down and over a bridge which crosses a tributary of Wellow Brook, then through woods.

Look out for a gap on the right, signposted as a Byway, leading to a footbridge across the stream. Cross here and follow the main track uphill.

You first reach a gate, then a junction where the right fork leads to Lower Baggridge. Keep straight on, through the gate ahead. You now bear right to follow the enclosed track to a gate and then a stone wall on your right as you approach the summit of the hill and the buildings of Upper Baggridge Farm.

From this high and windy ridge there is a fine view in all directions: east and south towards Salisbury Plain, Cley Hill and the woods of Longleat, across to Wellow and, a mile to the west of the village centre, on the sloping hillside and just below a small copse, the scar left by a vanished Roman villa. Up the valley to the west it is possible to see the pyramidal spoil heaps, now quite overgrown, and some villages associated with the long abandoned Somerset Coalfield.

From Upper Baggridge, follow the ridge-top lane for almost a mile in a south-westerly direction, until you reach a house on the edge of a wood. Here turn right along a wide track, signposted as a Byway, which descends the wooded hillside. This is a pretty half-mile walk.

As you emerge from the wood there is a the junction of ways. Here you turn right by the signposted Public Bridleway, with the hedgerow on your right. Walk past the ruined barn and head through the gate a little further along on your left. Now head downhill beside the hedge on your right to reach a gate.

Go through here and climb the hillside to reach a further gate in the top left corner. From here the way to Stoney Littleton Long

Barrow is visible a short distance to your left, lying within its fenced enclosure.

Stoney Littleton Long Barrow dates from the Bronze Age of four thousand years ago. It is an excellent example of a Cotswold-type long barrow which was used to inter members of the same family or clan over many generations. The door jambs (one of which displays a splendid ammonite cast) support a huge lintel and lead to three pairs of burial chambers on either side of a central gallery. It is quite possible to penetrate the farthest recesses of the ancient tomb, some fifty feet from the entrance, and to inspect the fine stonework of its construction.

Having explored the barrow, retrace your steps and turn left to follow the right of way back to Wellow. First you follow a hedge on your right, then carry on across an open field, then gradually descend by way of a hedged track to reach the lane where you bear left towards Wellow Brook. From here you retrace your steps to your starting point in the village.

Wellow bridge and ford

20 WESTWOOD

via Stowford, Farleigh Castle and Iford

Distance:	4 miles
Maps:	Pathfinders 1199, 1200; Explorer 5
	Landrangers 172, 173
Map Reference:	813590
Refreshment en route:	The New Inn at Westwood, the
	Hungerford Arms near Farleigh Castle.
	There are also tea rooms at Stowford,
	though opening times times vary.

THE WALK: Although an easy, short walk the route includes two manor houses, a beautiful parish church, a fifteenth century mill and a fourteenth century castle, a lost village, as well as a beautiful stretch of the River Frome. This really is a surprisingly lovely short ramble and, although the last in this book, should not be missed.

Westwood Manor and church make a fine group of ancient buildings on the edge of the village. The Manor belongs to the National Trust, has limited opening hours but is strongly recommended, though this may be subject to change. It is difficult to do justice to the Manor and church in a few lines, particularly as there are excellent guide books available on both.

Westwood Manor is a diminutive building, in comparison with Great Chalfield or South Wraxall, and has portions dating from c. 1400, the late fifteenth century and 1610. It was the rich clothier, Thomas Horton, who is commemorated in Holy Trinity Church in Bradford on Avon, who lived here and extended the house in the early 1600's. A fifteenth century stone barn is sited to the east of the Manor whilst the church of St. Mary is very close, being just to the south. The main feature of the church is its elaborate Somerset-type

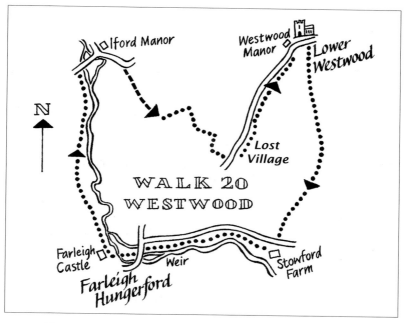

tower. The manor, especially, will repay a visit, when you may enjoy
a guided tour.

Opposite the Manor there is a National Trust car park; this makes a
convenient starting point for the walk. Look for the Public Footpath
signpost just beyond the car park. Cross the stile here and follow
the direction indicated by the sign towards Stowford, i.e. straight
across the field towards the clump of willows which surrounds a
small pond. Make for the stile to the left of the pond and climb over
into the next field.

Carry on in the same direction, straight ahead, until you reach
a stile in the hedgerow. Again, in the next field, walk ahead to reach
the crossing through the hedge. You can see Midway Manor away
to the left and Salisbury Plain in the distance ahead. Now follow
the beaten path, slightly downhill and veering gradually towards
the right. Simply walk on towards the group of old stone buildings
near the road; these are all in the vicinity of Stowford Farm.

Stowford Mill, according to Kenneth Rogers, was leased by one William Sewey, clothman, in 1458, from Keynsham Abbey, so it may have been used as a fulling mill from that date. Its most prosperous time was the fifteenth century when the present house was built. Stowford was used as a centre for the production of wool and cloth for four centuries; in the mid-nineteenth century it became a corn mill.

Cross the road with care and enter the driveway into Stowford Farm. The Countryside Commission, bless them, have recently negotiated the route of a permissive footpath which follows the riverside meadow from Stowford towards the bridge at Farleigh Hungerford. Its course is defined on the explanatory notice shown at the point where the field path from Iford meets the road opposite Stowford. According to this, the permissive footpath approaches the diving boards before the weir and then heads up the bank to meet the road, whence it is but a short distance to the bridge. Happily, you can walk on the grassy bank here so as to keep off the metalled surface of the road.

As you approach the buildings of Farleigh Hungerford in the river valley the road turns left over a pair of bridges which cross the River Frome and the mill stream respectively.

After the first bridge you can avoid the road up to the castle entrance by turning right before the pillar box and following the lane across the river to reach a point just below the ramparts of Farleigh Castle. You can bear left here and climb up to the castle entrance – this is also the way to go if you seek refreshment at the Hungerford Arms, a pub which is located just beyond the entrance to the castle.

An old mill stood on the island between the two waterways and was the last country mill to close down; a fulling mill was recorded here in 1548 which was worked until 1910.

Farleigh Castle is open to the public, at a price, and is maintained by English Heritage. A leaflet is obtainable, from which the following sketch is largely culled. The original castle dates from the 1370's and was built by Sir Thomas Hungerford, a Wiltshire squire who was Speaker of the House of Commons in 1377. He died in 1398 and is

Farleigh Castle

buried in an enormous tomb chest in the chapel within the castle. His son, Sir Walter Hungerford, also a Speaker of the House of Commons, extended the castle by adding an outer court to enclose the former parish church and built the new church of St. Leonard up the hill. Farleigh twice fell out of the possession of the Hungerfords and was twice repossessed. In the Civil War, the heir to Farleigh was commander of the Parliamentary forces in Wiltshire, and defeated his Royalist half-brother who had formerly occupied the castle. A later Hungerford, known as 'The Spendthrift', sold Farleigh in 1686, and it passed through various hands until placed under the guardianship of the Ministry of Works in 1919.

To continue the walk: follow the track towards the Trout Farm and look out for the Footpath sign on the right which directs you across a plank bridge toward a stile. Once across this stile you bear right to follow the river bank through several fields until you reach the lane at Iford. This is a wonderful stretch, but remember to look back towards the castle and the tower of Farleigh Hungerford church.

There is a second weir at Iford which once controlled the flow of a mill stream that powered the former Iford Mill. The iron sluice gates can be seen at the head of the mill stream.

Turn right at the lane past the former mill and over the bridge to Iford Manor (for description see Walk 1).

From Iford Manor turn right up the hill. Turn off onto the signposted bridleway, the entrance to which you find a little way uphill on your right. This shady track climbs gently above the valley of the River Frome, and offers some lovely views through gaps in the hedge.

The track eventually meets a stream and continues on the far side. Your route, however, requires you to cross the stream and then the stile immediately on your left to enter a field. Now follow the left hand boundary of the field. Ignore the track which bears off to the left beside the sewage works but keep to the beaten path along the field edge. Soon you turn through a right angle to the right, climb a little, then turn to the left, then right again, but always with the hedgerow on your left.

Eventually you will reach a narrow, hedged-in track in the top corner of the last field; take this to reach the lane which connects Farleigh Hungerford with Westwood, but first look back towards the village of Westwood, situated on the hill-top to the north, and down the valley of the River Frome toward Monkton Combe and the mushroom-like water tower on Bathampton Down.

Turn left at the lane and enter the field opposite by a stile. This field, and the one on the far side of the lane, constitute the site of the lost medieval village of Rowley. It is well worth entering this field to step across its hummocky surface. Somewhere towards the field's centre is a long hollowed-out stretch which it is tempting to believe was the village main street.

There is an exit from this field in the far left corner. From here you have the choice either of walking back to Westwood along the lane, which is generally very quiet, or negotiating the field path which runs parallel to the lane and just inside the hedgerow.

If you choose the green way, then climb over the stile to enter the next field on the right and follow the hedge toward Westwood Church. You can continue in this direction all the way back to the stile at which you began this walk, close to the little car park opposite the entrance to Westwood Manor.

Phew !

More books from Ex Libris Press:

EXPLORING HISTORIC WILTSHIRE: Volumes 1 & 2
This major new work focuses on twelve of the finest rural landscapes in Wiltshire.

Volume 1 deals with the north of the county and includes Ridgeway Country; The Central Marlborough Downs; Wansdyke; Grigson Country; Calstone, Oldbury and Roundway Down; The Vale of Pewsey.

Volume 2 covers the south of the county to include Chute Causeway; The Wylye Valley; Wiltshire Selwood & White Sheet Downs; Great Ridge & Grovely Woods; The South Wiltshire Ridgeways; South-East Wiltshire.

Each book contains 176 pages and is illustrated throughout with a mixture of black and white photographs, sketch maps and line drawings.
Both are priced at £7.95

THE PROSPECT OF WILTSHIRE
Words by John Chandler; pictures by Jim Lowe; maps by Karen Pigott
The first and only full-colour book dedicated to the beauties of this special county.
112 pages; full colour photographs and maps throughout; Price £14.95

BRADFORD VOICES
A Study of Bradford on Avon through the Twentieth Century
by Margaret Dobson
'...a remarkable social history. It is scholarly and reliable, detailed but never dull, and it flows seamlessly and fairly, through all the events and issues of Bradford's recent past, bringing them (and us) firmly into the present.'
256 pages; illustrated throughout; Price £9.95

A SENSE OF BELONGING
History, Community and the New Wiltshire
by John Chandler
128 pages; Price £5.95

PEDLARS PACK
1 A BATH ASSORTMENT
2 A SALISBURY ASSORTMENT
Small format books on English towns, each Pedlar's Pack volume is a mini-anthology and a perfect keepsake of particular places.
Each is 80 pages, illustrated with line drawings and priced at £3.95

COUNTRY BOOKSHELF from Ex Libris Press:

LAND GIRL by Anne Hall
Her story of six years in the
Women's Land Army, 1940-46
*144 pages; Illustrated throughout;
Price £4.95*

LUMBER JILL by Mavis Williams
Her story of four years in the
Women's Timber Corps, 1942-45
96 pages; Illustrated; Price £3.95

VILLAGE PRACTICE by Anne
Stratford
A Year in the life of a Country
Doctor's Wife
160 pages; Illustrated; Price £4.95

POACHERS & POISONED OWLS
by Romy Wyeth
Tales of a Country Policeman's Wife
96 pages; Illustrated; Price £4.50

WINIFRED by Sylvia Marlow
Her childhood and early working life
*128 pages; Illustrated throughout;
Price £4.50*

MAISIE & ME by Stella Ashton
A Country Childhood in the 1920s
80 pages; pen & ink drawings; Price £3.95

THE ROMANY WAY by Irene Soper
112 pages; Fully illustrated ; Price £4.95

MY NEW FOREST HOME
by Irene Soper
128 pages; Illustrated; Price £4.95

GROWING WITH THE GRAIN
A farming story by Richard Mack
160 pages; Illustrated; Price £4.95

O WHO WILL MARRY ME?
A Book of Country Love
by Ralph Whitlock
*80 pages; Illustrated with engravings;
Price £3.50*

**MARCH WINDS &
APRIL SHOWERS**
Country Weather Lore
by Ralph Whitlock
*80 pages; Illustrated with Bewick
engravings; Price £3.50*

**LETTERS FROM THE ENGLISH
COUNTRYSIDE**
by Ralph Whitlock
*160 pages; Numerous pen & ink drawings;
Price £4.95*

THE SECRET LANE: *A Country Story*
Ralph Whitlock's only published novel
160 pages; Price £4.95

**CHRISTIANA AWDRY'S
HOUSEHOLD BOOK**
by Margaret Jensen
*128 pages; Pen & ink drawings;
Price £4.95*

**GRAN'S OLD-FASHIONED
REMEDIES, WRINKLES AND RECIPES**
by Jean Penny
*96 pages; Numerous engravings;
Price £3.50*

**GRAN'S OLD-FASHIONED
GARDENING GEMS**
by Jean Penny
*96 pages; Numerous engravings;
Price £3.50*

*These books may be obtained through your
local bookshop or direct from the publisher,
post-free, at*

1 The Shambles
Bradford on Avon
Wiltshire BA15 1JS.
Tel/Fax 01225 863595

Please ask for our free illustrated list.